DOWSING

DENNIS WHEATLEY

Thorsons

Thorsons
An Imprint of HarperCollins*Publishers*
77–85 Fulham Palace Road,
Hammersmith, London W6 8JB

The Thorsons website address is: www.thorsons.com

Published by Thorsons 2000

1 3 5 7 9 10 8 6 4 2

A catalogue record for this book
is available from the British Library

ISBN 0 7225 4029 9

Printed and bound in Great Britain by
Omnia Books Limited, Glasgow

CONTENTS

TO THOSE DOWSERS WHO INFLUENCED MY DOWSING PERCEPTIONS – GUY UNDERWOOD, TOM LETHBRIDGE, DR J HAVELOCK FIDLER AND HAMISH MILLER.

ALSO TO BERNHARD, A GERMAN MASTER-DOWSER WHO PACED THE ANCIENT SITES WITH ME, REVEALED INCREDIBLE NEW DOWSING DIMENSIONS, AND PERSUADED ME TO PUT PEN TO PAPER.

PREFACE

When I first started to dowse, there was still a school of thought existing that one should not teach anyone to dowse, apart from demonstrating the first elementary reaction of dowsing rods or pendulums. The idea was that the beginner had to find out everything for him- or herself, from their own 'inner teacher' and not absorb ideas or concepts from other people.

This 'hard line' had a certain truth in it, but it meant very few people could, or were prepared to, venture into an apprenticeship in the art of dowsing. However, over recent years, things have changed dramatically. There are now advanced dowsing tutors ready to impart to beginners not only the dowsing rudiments but also a much wider knowledge which can only be acquired by extensive study and years of practice.

One of these highly advanced teachers is Dennis Wheatley. Some of his teachings have developed from the works of the late Guy Underwood who discovered the geodetic system of earth energies, as well as from later exponents of other earth energy systems.

This book is a comprehensive guide for both novices and experienced dowsers alike. None of us can become experts in all of the fields of dowsing but, gradually, we find an area of the discipline that really appeals to us, and which works well for us. It is at this stage that our 'inner teacher' takes over and we discover things that are especially meaningful.

So, even this truly excellent book – comprehensive though it is – is not the full story of dowsing. No book can ever make that claim. But once you have read it and feel attracted by its contents, you will, no doubt, be influenced to progress in your own way. This is the author's main message. 'We do not use dowsing,' said Enid Smithett, a well-known exponent of the art, 'Dowsing uses us!'

So, let Dennis Wheatley become your guide and this book your reference. And move on from there.

SIR CHARLES JESSEL, BT.

PAST PRESIDENT AND HONORARY LIFE VICE PRESIDENT
OF THE BRITISH SOCIETY OF DOWSERS

DOWSING PERCEPTIONS

Dowsing is popularly associated with water finding, conjuring up visions of old men using Y-shaped twigs which mysteriously react when approaching a water supply in the earth. Down the ages there have been many celebrated water diviners. Such dowsers exist today with incredible skills. George Applegate finds water supplies when dowsing from aircraft and has not made a mistake in 15 years. But the scope of dowsing is much wider than water finding.

SO, WHAT IS DOWSING?

Dowsing can be simply defined as the skill of detecting invisible targets. This being so, its scope is limited only by the imagination. For example, some dowsers specialise in the following fields:

Water	Oil	Gas Supplies
Mineral Lodes	Soil Analysis	Precious Metals
Archaeological Remains	Treasure Troves	Medical Diagnosis
Finding Lost Objects	Finding Lost People	Map Dowsing

The list could be extended indefinitely.

Many dowsers are adept at finding earth energy flows and exotic patterns, which interlace the surface of the planet. On a more prosaic level, underground public utilities – from water pipes to sewers – can be accurately located by dowsing.

SO, HOW DOES ONE DOWSE?

Most people need to dowse with a dowsing tool such as an L-rod or pendulum as shown in the illustration.

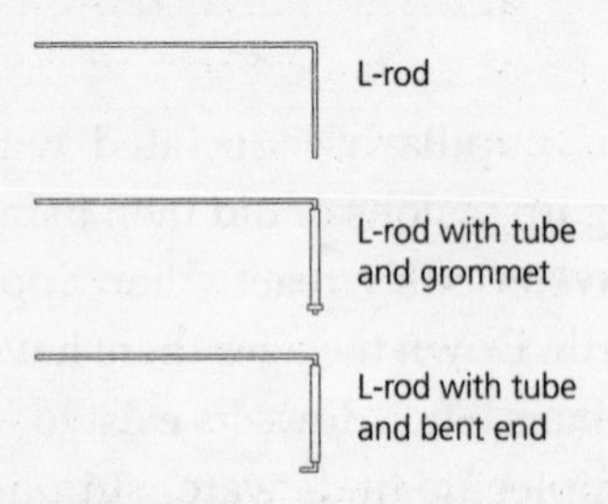

Angle rods and pendulums. The rod can be made from a metal coat hanger, piano wire or fencing wire. The tube can be of metal or plastic such as a ballpoint pen casing. Tube retention can be achieved by bending the rod's end or using a grommet, as shown. A pendulum can be made of wood, crystal, brass or perspex in weights from 2.5g to 10g. The cord can be a fine twine or chain.

Dowsing tools act as 'indicators' when a dowsing target is found. An L-rod will swivel and a pendulum will gyrate. The dowsing tools do not respond to the target. The body reacts to the target and the dowsing tools respond to a dowsing reflex mechanism. Theories abound as to what the dowsing mechanism is. These we will discuss later.

L-rods are easy to make from wire coat hangers, piano or fencing wire. A pendulum can be of any weight, the bob being from 2½ to 10 grams, suspended on a fine cord, twine or chain.

Some dowsers need no dowsing tools and this is known as device-less dowsing. They intuitively 'sense' the target or may have tingling feelings in their body.

THE SIXTH SENSE

Dowsing is a form of sixth sense latent in all of us which has atrophied in modern man. After all, why dowse for water when it is on tap in the home? Guy Underwood believed the dowsing sixth sense to be an 'atavism' inherited from our remote ancestors, the early tool-making hominids to whom it was invaluable in the evolutionary survival stakes.

Most people do not realize they have this sixth sense but it can be easily triggered and, with practice, developed to professional standards. In over 10 years of teaching dowsing, I have not found a person who could not dowse. Children adapt to dowsing much more easily than adults as they carry less mental baggage, biases and prejudices. They learn rapidly and often make faster progress than adults. From the onset they believe the dowsing rods will work for them. Adults often do not have this approach and have inner doubts as to their dowsing potential.

Tom Lethbridge, the doyen of long-cord pendulum dowsing, believed that everyone could dowse and the few who could not had simply 'blown a psychic fuse'. He also believed that a piece of chewing gum on the end of a string was more powerful than all the world's supercomputers as it put the holder in touch with the higher self which knows the answers to all questions.

Edgar Cayce, the American dowser, seer and healer, spoke of accessing 'The Akashic Record', a cosmic library of total knowledge. His grandfather taught him to dowse at the age of four. He learnt the skill rapidly and his grandfather said: 'Edgar, one day you will be quite famous!' He was.

WHAT IS THE DOWSING MECHANISM?

Let's look at some recent research into the dowsing mechanism:

THE BODY SENSORS

Dr Zaboj Harvalik, an American scientist, researched a German master dowser, Wilhelm De Boere, a highly sensitive dowser. De Boere was asked to dowse a high-frequency energy beam – to him the simplest of tasks. De Boere found he could not dowse when Dr Harvalik placed metal discs over his pineal gland and adrenal glands. Harvalik's series of elegant experiments revealed an aspect of the dowsing reaction never before explored. A link between these glands and the dowsing reflex was established, but there were other dimensions that awaited research. The brain was involved in the dowsing equation.

BRAIN WAVE ACTIVITIES

In the 1980s Dr Edith Jurka, MD, an American, recorded the brain wave activities of dowsers using a 'mind mirror' developed by Dr C Maxwell-Cade based on electroencephalographs (EEG). She found some remarkable correlations in brain-wave activity associated with dowsing. When in the dowsing mode the brain wave beta frequency of the thinking state lowers in frequency to the alpha state which is a meditative state. When a dowsing target is found there is a burst of the lower frequency theta state of around 4 to 7 cycles per second, which corresponds to brain wave activity in dreaming sleep.

More recently, in 1996, a team headed by Edward Stillman, the scientific adviser to the American Dowsing Society, investigated brain wave activity of dowsers, using modern computer-controlled EEG equipment which can generate coloured pictures. This research confirmed Dr Jurka's findings and broke new ground on this subject.

Human brain wave activities covering deep unbroken sleep to the waking state are shown below. (Hz = cycles per second):

Frequency	**Relative Consciousness Levels**
Beta above 14 Hz	The conscious waking state of processing information
Alpha 8 to 13 Hz	Reflective, contemplating, restful. The dowsing mental mode.
Theta 4 to 7 Hz	Dreaming sleep
Delta 0.5 to 3Hz	Deep, dreamless sleep

- In Transcendental meditation alpha and theta waves are present.
- In Zen meditation, beta, alpha and theta waves are present.
- In dowsing, beta, alpha and theta waves are present.

Edward Stillman, commenting on the latest research, said: 'Dowsing appears to be a truly unique and creative human altered state of consciousness.'

THE LEFT AND RIGHT BRAIN HEMISPHERES

There has also been the suggestion that dowsing is associated with connections between the right and left parts of the brain. The left part is concerned with logic, reasoning and coping with all sensual impressions. The right brain is the 'intuitive' side, providing insight and inspiration.

Mozart said that the music seemed 'to walk through his head'. Did he mean an inspirational transfer of melodies from the right to the left brain for processing into musical scores?

As dowsing is hardly a logical skill, does the inspiration come from the right brain – Lethbridge's 'higher self'?

As we shall see, in dowsing we need to be in the contemplative

alpha state and cease the activity of the left brain as much as we can.

RADIATIONS

Alf Riggs, a British dowser and researcher into the energy-depleting state of ME, found that underground water molecules travelling at over two miles per hour, interact with the strata they move through and in the process generate the following phenomena:

- A positive vertical electrical field
- A DC magnetic field
- Radio frequencies
- High energy waves in a 6 cm band at the stream's centre
- Ultra-short waves in 6 cm bands at both edges

Could it be that water diviners react to some or all of these phenomena, intuitively, via the right brain?

As a boy, the famous French dowser, Barthelemy Bléton, became violently sick over underground streams: maybe he was allergic to this cocktail of radiations. A dowser noted Barthelemy was always sick over a certain location. He dowsed the location and discovered an underground stream. The boy's reaction to this underground current was a form of 'deviceless dowsing'.

THE DOWSON

Dr Vincent Reddish revealed in *Physics Works*, May 1995, a dowsing phenomenon he called the 'D-Field', associated with a hitherto unknown particle he named the 'dowson'.

He had detected interference fringe patterns created by the interaction of radiation fields with linear structures on the ground and above it. The energetic waves generated charges on the ground which are conducted through a dowser's body. He called this the 'D-Force' which involved the dowson particles. He concluded that dowsing signals were neither magnetic, electromagnetic nor gravitational in nature. This may be an over-generalization as we shall discover in chapter 4, 'Earth Energies', patterns which are electromagnetic in nature.

DOWSING ENIGMAS

None of the above theories can explain map dowsing for mineral lodes thousands of miles away or how a water diviner can assess the flow rate in litres per hour of an invisible stream, and also decide on its potability.

The water diviner, if shown a surface stream, would not be able to comment on its flow rate. He establishes these parameters by 'information dowsing' – one of the great dowsing enigmas we shall investigate.

Map dowsing is also one of dowsing's great mysteries and is a form of 'distant' dowsing. Poring over a map with a pendulum then finding sources of water, oil or gas in a far-off location suggests some form of communication with the 'higher self' – the superconsciousness which knows the answers to all questions. Map dowsing techniques will be discussed later.

DOWSING HISTORY

Dowsing has a long history. In a French cave are neolithic carvings of dowsing tools – referred to as 'The Library of Dowsing Tools'. The American dowser, Sig Lonegren, reported on cave art in Tassili, Algeria, in which a character holds a dowsing tool and is watched by onlookers. Was he giving a dowsing lesson, one wonders? The art has been dated to 6000 BC.

Dowsers are depicted on ancient Egyptian bas-reliefs, and Cleopatra is reputed to have employed dowsers to find gold. Dowsers appear on a statue of the Chinese Emperor Kwang Su, who reigned around 2200 BC.

Agricola's book *De Re Metallica* (1550) includes an illustration of dowsers prospecting for minerals.

A great deal of dowsing information and methods came from France and were the work of bishops, abbés and priests, despite the church hierarchy denouncing dowsing as the work of the Devil. Clearly, these clerics thought otherwise and decided to 'publish and be damned!'

During the Second World War, the Nazis created a dowsing academy in Munich with dowsers and scientists combining their talents to further the war effort. As the allies marched on Munich, the Nazis stripped the academy of all research data – nothing is known of the activities except a reference to a new force called 'the X-force', which was discovered by the physicists Wüste and Wimmer, working with dowsers.

The American General Patton employed dowsers during World War Two to locate underground water supplies in arid regions.

During the Vietnam War the American military created a dowsing school to train the marines in dowsing countermeasures against the Vietcong guerrilla fighters. The Vietcong tactic was to strike suddenly, then vanish into foxholes and networks of underground tunnels or behind false walls in village houses. They also set deadly and varied booby traps.

The dowsing school replicated a typical Vietnamese village with underground networks, booby traps and houses with false walls. The marines were trained to use L-rods to locate tunnels and to count how many people occupied the tunnels. They also became skilled in detecting hidden booby traps. So, for the American marines, the dowsing rod became a weapon of war.

Captured guerrilla fighters must have wondered how the marines found them hiding in tunnels or behind false walls in village houses.

During the 20th century dowsing societies grew. In 1933 Colonel AH Bell formed the British Society of Dowsers and held the elected post of president through to 1964. By 1999 there were 21 separate dowsing societies in Britain – many affiliated to the BSD. Since its inception only two presidents have been civilians. The rest are military men of various ranks to Major General.

The American Society of Dowsers Inc is the world's largest dowsing society and has 75 affiliated dowsing chapters. A list of worldwide dowsing societies is given in 'Addresses of Interest' at the end of the book.

In the old Soviet Union, dowsing was taken even more seriously, and a master's degree in dowsing could be obtained from several universities. There the term 'dowsing' was replaced by the 'bioplasmic method' and dowsers were called 'operators'. The Russian operators in particular were astounded that dowsing was not highly regarded in the western world. Only recently has Cambridge university accepted that water dowsing works, and this after years of scepticism.

The interest in dowsing has grown almost exponentially over the past fifty years and has reached maturity. This is borne out by the fact that dowsing has been embraced by UNESCO, the Canadian ministry of agriculture, the Czech army and major corporations worldwide. Additionally, thousands of doctors complement their work by diagnostic dowsing and appropriate treatment with homoeopathy or Bach flower remedies.

Some dowsers concentrate solely on medical diagnostics. The body scientific has always been sceptical about dowsing but doesn't bother to investigate the subject. It is hardly scientific to have an opinion on a subject without, first, researching it.

FAMOUS NAMES IN DOWSING

Some of the most famous people in history were dowsers, including: Leonardo Da Vinci, Robert Boyle (the founder of the Royal Society), Sir Isaac Newton, Johan Ritter (the founding father of electrochemistry) Thomas Edison and Albert Einstein.

In 1897, Sir JJ Thomson made one of the greatest scientific discoveries when he isolated the electron. The control of the electron has transformed the 20th century with dazzling technologies from computers to television receivers. For this, Thomson was knighted and given the Nobel Prize. During a presentation to a group of eminent scientists he requested that science should turn its attention to the physics of dowsing – but this plea fell on deaf ears. To JJ Thompson, dowsing was for real!

MENTAL DOWSING PRINCIPLES

We have seen that dowsing is associated with mental states and that the brain-wave patterns register these. Also that 'spiritual' dimensions were introduced by Tom Lethbridge and Edgar Cayce, linking dowsing with the higher self – the source of cosmic knowledge – whilst Underwood regarded dowsing as the activation of the 'sixth sense'.

Later, in 1986, the American dowser, Sig Lonegren, introduced the concept of 'spiritual dowsing'.

Dowsing, in effect, involves both physical activity, such as the use of dowsing tools, and mental activity. The latter is of paramount importance since without mental preparation, there can be no dowsing.

So, what is the secret, if that is the word, in activating the dowsing 'sixth-sense'? The answer lies in 'visualization' and 'frame of mind'. We will examine these in some detail. In effect they are simple precepts.

VISUALIZATION

In the dowsing discipline the first law is, simply, *'you will not detect that which you cannot visualize'*. In other words, if you do not know what you seek, you will never find it!

There is a vital need to visualize a dowsing target to the best of one's ability. Some targets are easy to visualize, such as water and gas pipes or electrical wiring in walls. Lost objects such as car keys and wallets are, likewise, easy to visualize.

In visualizing any target, it is important to *hold this visualization in the mind to the exclusion of everything else.* In this one-pointed visualization you are completely 'tuning in' to the target, and 'tuning out' the rest of the universe. Nothing but the target must exist for you.

VARIATIONS OF VISUALIZATION

Visualization varies in people just as the senses vary. Some people attain excellent mental images whilst others find visualization difficult.

Major General WF Cooper, the present President of the British Society of Dowsers, has an important truth to impart in dowsing. *'Intent is all'*.

So, if you are not adept at visualization, don't be over-concerned. Keep the *thought* of the target uppermost in the mind to the exclusion of all else. Let this be your intent. Here, intent means that, although you may be deficient in visualizing, you can still find another way of 'tuning in' to your target which will be equally effective.

INTANGIBLE TARGETS

In later chapters, we shall examine earth energies and aerial ley energies, which are intangible entities. The 'Michael' and 'Mary' earth energy rivers course from Land's End to the Norfolk coast and can be up to 22 paces wide. So, how does one visualize these two vast earth energy rivers?

One method I have taught over the years has worked successfully and students were able to detect the two rivers in their first attempts. Simply visualize 'Michael' as a scintillating river of silver and 'Mary' as a scintillating river of blue. By making them mentally visible we can then proceed to detect their leading and trailing edges, or track their undulating courses.

Aerial ley energy passes between standing stones on ley lines and between all stones in a circle, so visualize this energy as a linear silver beam. Try to use this or your own methods of visualization for invisible intangible energies.

WITNESSES

Some dowsing books advocate the use of 'samples' of the target or 'witnesses' to enhance the visualization. If, for example, water is the target, then they advise holding a bottle of water in the hand so that it touches the palm and the rod. If the target is a water pipe then a piece of steel or plastic similar to the pipe is held.

With good visualization, however, enhancing witnesses are not needed.

FRAME OF MIND

Note how long it takes for professional ball players such as golfers, tennis players, and snooker players, to achieve the *right 'frame of mind'* before they strike. They attune themselves bodily and mentally for the strike and visualize their bodily movements and what will happen to the ball along a trajectory or, in the case of a snooker player, what will happen to the ball struck, and where the white ball will eventually come to rest. When professional players shape up badly in a tournament they

invariably offer as the reason *'I wasn't in the right "frame of mind".'* We can learn from these ball-playing professionals.

To achieve the right dowsing *'frame of mind'*, one has to apply a few simple precepts before *every* dowsing task. With practice these simple precepts will become 'second nature' to you. They are:

- Relax, bodily and mentally, take a couple of deep breaths, and let your arms hang loosely by your sides.
- Eliminate all butterfly thoughts; still the mind; bury the ego.
- Visualize the target in quiet concentration. But, importantly, don't 'over-concentrate' as this will lead to either no results or, at best, spurious results.
- Be quietly confident that the rods will work for you, but *never* be 'over-confident'. Dowsing cockiness produces inconsistent results. Dowsing rods act, at times, as if they have a mind of their own and can play tricks – as we shall see. They are great ego-tamers.
- Eliminate from your mind all preconceived notions, biases, autosuggestion; and never predict what the rods will do. Should you do this, the rods will willingly oblige by reacting as you predicted.
- Be a totally neutral observer of events with no interest whatsoever in whether the rods will react at any point.
- Make your dowsing passes slowly. Dowse like a sporting action replay and allow the rods to overcome their inertia on finding a target.
- Should a sudden noise interrupt your dowsing *'frame of mind'* – a passing truck, helicopter, or voices – abandon the dowsing pass and re-establish your *'frame of mind'*.
- Don't dowse if you are feeling low with flu or some other complaint, or when fatigued.

- Dowsing can be fatiguing so dowse in short periods followed by relaxation breaks. A suitable routine could be, for example, fifteen minutes dowsing with a ten-minute relaxation break.
- If you visit an ancient site to dowse for, say, earth energy patterns, don't begin dowsing immediately. If you have journeyed by car, you will probably be stressed. Each site has its own 'persona' or 'spirit of place' so, on arrival, relax for fifteen minutes and quietly absorb the ambience and feel of the place.
- Don't be over-serious about dowsing. It's great fun, so enjoy it!

In the precepts described we are faced with an apparent contradiction in talking of 'relaxation' and 'concentration' simultaneously. Hamish Miller neatly sums dowsing up in his phrase *'relaxed concentration'*.

SPIRITUAL DOWSING

In his book *Spiritual Dowsing*, Sig Lonegren equates dowsing with spiritual dimensions. If dowsing puts one in touch with the *'higher self'*, or the *'superconsciousness'* then due respect must be paid to whatever power is involved. In other words, the blasé approach tinged with ego is discarded in the spiritual approach.

Sig advocates that, prior to any dowsing task, three questions should be asked. If three *'yes'* responses are obtained, he proceeds with the dowsing task. If a single *'no'* response is received then he does not proceed.

'Can I?' asks the question 'Am I ready for the task?'
'Should I?' means 'Am I right to proceed now?'
'May I?' requests permission to proceed.

A 'no' response to 'Should I?' may mean *now* is not the right time.

Later, we will discuss the programming of rods and pendulums to give 'yes' and 'no' responses in information dowsing.

DOWSING ETHICS

'Information Dowsing' can provide answers to an infinite variety of questions. If the answers emanate from the higher self one must then be highly circumspect in the use of any knowledge gained.

Never use 'Information Dowsing' for personal gain or self-aggrandizement. Do not use the information for gambling be it lotteries, horse racing or predicting soccer results: instead of acquiring wealth, you could find your assets slipping away. If employed as a dowser for a company or person, do not think of gain but charge a fair fee for the service. Leave behind a 'feel good' factor.

In teaching dowsing I am paid a fee by the Education Authorities. This is not profiteering from dowsing. I give a service and am paid the same fees as teachers of other subjects such as languages and mathematics. The only difference between us is that I know I have an easier teaching task and have no homework-marking chores.

I once carried out a dowsing job for a construction company with water problems at one of their buildings. I sorted out the problem in around 30 minutes. The managing director was delighted and asked me what my fee was. I said that it would be 70 miles of petrol and, for the 30 minutes work, £10. This surprised him. They had worked without success on the problem for over a week. He expected my fee to be hundreds of pounds. He wrote out a cheque, which I didn't look at. Later, having arrived home, I found it was for £100.

PHYSICAL DOWSING PRINCIPLES

We will now examine the physical dowsing principles of using L-rods and pendulums and their reactions to target detection. In the exercises which follow, use sleeved rods since this not only eliminates skin friction by insulating the hands from the rods, but allows the rods to swivel freely. Either purchase a set of rods from the dowsing societies listed under 'Addresses of Interest' at the end of the book, or make them from steel coat hangers, fencing wire or piano wire. The sleeves can be made from ballpoint pen casings. Pendulums can be purchased from the Societies or homemade.

Aeroplane model shops generally stock a wide selection of piano wire in different diameters as well as copper and brass tubes in different diameters for sleeves. They also stock brass grommets for holding the sleeves 'in situ'.

ROD HANDLING

Hold the rod tubes in either hand with a pistol-type grip. Don't grip too tightly but have a relaxed hold. For the best operation of the rods, note carefully the following:

a The upper arms and forearms should form a right angle and the forearms should be parallel to the ground.
b The rods should be separated by the body's width.
c The rods should be parallel to each other and to the floor. Should they point upwards they tend to become unstable in proportion to the angle made with the ground. If the rods point to the ground, this interferes with rod movement.

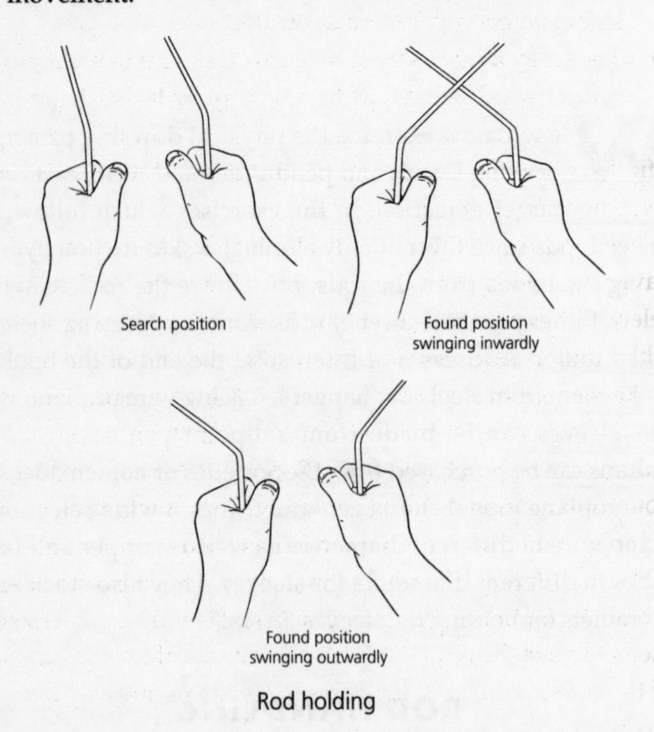

Rod holding

Practise swivelling the rods from side to side in unison to get the 'feel' of rod movements. Now practise walking with the rods parallel to each other and to the ground. This is known as the 'search' or 'prospecting' mode. You will, very quickly, master the art of walking with the rods in 'search'.

THE 'FOUND' REACTION

On finding a dowsing target the rods may swivel out of the 'search' mode in the ways shown in the illustration.

- The rods may swing, simultaneously, inwards and come to rest crossed after a 45° movement.
- They may swing inwardly by more than 45° and may even swing far enough to rest across the body.
- They may move away from each other as if being repulsed. The outward swing may be anything up to 180 degrees.

I find that many of my American students have an outward swing instead of inwardly crossing.

The 'found' position is different for each individual so you have to establish what *your* own 'found' mode is. To do this, select a visible target. This could be the edge of a path, lawn or table edge. Take time to get into the right frame of mind, visualize the target, and make a slow dowsing pass with the rods in 'search' towards it, at right angles, and from about four feet (1.2m) away. On reaching the target the rods will swivel into 'found'. Whatever the position, this is your 'found' mode.

In this exercise, you are more concerned with *what* the rods will *do* rather than establishing, with any degree of accuracy, the actual target. Let us assume your 'found' mode is crossed rods, then where is the target? Is it directly under the crossing points of the rods? Beneath your feet? Somewhere midway between the two?

ACCURACY

This is where accuracy enters the equation. To locate a target accurately one needs an accuracy reference point. This could be, for example, the tip of the right thumb. If you select this reference point then simply command the rods to swing to 'found' when the thumb tip is aligned with the target. Now make another dowsing pass across the selected target and note that the rods respond as the position of your thumb tip coincides with the target. This is 'rod programming'.

WIDE TARGETS

In the case of wide targets, such as the 'Michael' or 'Mary' currents, or, say, a sewer pipe, pick up the leading edge using your accuracy reference, then set the rods in 'search' again, and continue the dowsing pass to identify the trailing edge.

SMALLER TARGETS

An accuracy reference can also be the tip of a needle or skewer. For example, in trying to locate electric wiring in a wall, you need some form of accuracy indicator that you can use with the free hand. You may wish to hang a picture but do not want to drive a nail into an electric wire.

At the point selected for the picture, tune in to electric cabling and use a single dowsing rod. With a skewer, or needle, in your free hand, programme the rod to react when the skewer or needle tip is coincident with the wire. Now move the tip around the area which will receive the picture hanger. If the rod reacts, select another spot and repeat the procedure. In later chapters we will dowse for a variety of phenomena.

INFORMATION DOWSING

Rods can be programmed to give 'yes' or 'no' responses. Simply put the rods into 'search' and give the polite command, 'Show me a "yes" response.' Repeat the procedure with, 'Show me a "no" response.' As in establishing your 'found' mode, the rod will decide for you what these responses are. For example, crossed rods for 'yes' and repulsed rods for 'no', or vice-versa. Once established, these responses will be constant for the rest of your life but, at this stage, you must heed a caveat. The rods can act capriciously for reasons unknown and, occasionally, will switch the yes/no responses for a day or so, and then revert back to the original mode. Unless this is recognized, you could invoke spurious answers. So, a vital rule in 'information dowsing' is that, prior to seeking answers, you must always check that your original yes/no responses prevail. It only takes a matter of seconds to confirm a 'yes' response, for example.

With rods programmed to give 'yes' and 'no' responses, one can enter the infinite world of information dowsing, answering questions even of an abstract nature, finding lost objects or seeking directions. Imagine all of the possible questions your mind can conjure up. You could, as a first experiment, begin by laying down a line of household commodities such as an apple, boot polish, a pear, furniture polish, lemonade, bread, detergent powder, cheese, and washing-up liquid, then asking the question, at each item, 'Is this commodity capable of being easily digested by me?' Note the answers. Were they correct?

TRICK ANSWERS

So far we have examined several pitfalls in dowsing, from over-concentration to over-confidence and the loss of that all-important aspect, the correct 'frame of mind'. In 'relaxed concentration' we must realize that it is up to ourselves to create that sense of 'balance' in concentration and confidence but the capricious rods may enter into the dowsing equation in more ways than one. We now recognize that our constant yes/no responses can switch, sporadically and transiently, but what if the rods provide 'trick' answers? How would we identify an answer as being true, or false? Do the rods really have a mind of their own and revel in the taming of egos?

Tom Graves, one of the most prolific authors on dowsing, recognized this trait in rods and pendulums and called trick answers 'Hermes' responses! Hermes was one of the Olympian pantheon of gods and amongst his many talents was trickery.

So, how does one sort out the true from the false? Simply use information dowsing and ask the question 'Is this a trick response?' and note the answer. 'Yes, this is a trick response', or 'no, it is not!' Once they have been rumbled, the rods will come clean!

So, with these examples of a rod's capriciousness, it behoves us not to have unbridled faith in the dowsing instruments, be they rods or pendulums, and always check responses. Verify a response once only. As an experiment, I tried verifying a questionable response several times and received the 'yes' reply four times. On the fifth time the rods suddenly reverted to 'no'. It is as if the rods had wearied of this constant probing and, eventually, decided to confuse persistent questioners. They have a short fuse in toleration.

ASK THE RIGHT QUESTION

The art of successful dowsing is, simply, asking the right question. Always try to make the question short, crystal clear, and never ask double answer questions such as, for example, 'Is X big and black?' What is big – an elephant, a planet, a star or a galaxy? If size is important relate the question to metric or imperial measurement units. 'Is X over 500 metres in depth?' 'Yes'. 'Is it over 800 metres in depth?' 'No'. So it is in between, and now you can home in on the depth. 'Is it 510, 520, 530 metres?' and so on. Suppose you wish to know a standing stone's date of erection. If you ask the question 'How old is this stone?' and start counting backwards from, say, 1000 BC in units of 50 years ... 1050, 1100, 1150, etc, be prepared to stand around for weeks or months on end as the stone may have had its genesis countless millions of years ago. The correct question would be: 'When was this stone placed in this location?' If you ask a vague, ill-defined question, don't expect a crystal clear answer.

ROD REACTIONS IN COUNT EXERCISES

In counting exercises the rods are held in the 'search' mode, parallel with each other and the ground. As the counting proceeds, the rods will remain in 'search' but as the target count is neared, the rods swing inwardly by a few degrees. This means you are getting close! Keep on counting and the rods will gradually inch nearer to the 'found' position when the correct count is reached.

DIRECTIONAL DOWSING

Many books on dowsing cover this technique as 'dynamic dowsing'. To find the direction of an object, place, or compass point in dynamic dowsing, use a single rod held in the 'search' alignment, pointing forwards away from your body. The rod should be parallel with the ground. Now with your free hand outstretched and your index finger pointing to the horizon as an indicator visualize the target and slowly rotate the body through 360 degrees with your finger scanning the horizon. When the finger aligns with the target, the rod will swing to the 'found' position as if it is working in unison with a rod held in the other hand. There is, however, a simpler method of directional dowsing which I discovered a few years ago. Whilst relaxing on my garden patio, I picked up a dowsing rod I had

left by the chair on the previous day. I put it into 'search' and said 'Show me the direction of the greenhouse'. The rod swivelled in that direction. I then pinpointed a score of items in the garden, including individual plant species and shrubs. I call this 'static directional dowsing' since it involves no bodily movements. The rod does the work.

PRACTICE

As an initial exercise, sit in one room of your home and hold the rod in 'search'. Then ask to be shown a variety of objects, in turn, such as a television set, a wall switch, wall light, door, window, a painting, a photograph or a statue. Now graduate to invisible objects in the garden if you have one, or in another room. In a garden, target a shed, a greenhouse or individual trees and other features. In another room, for example, it could be the direction of a cooker, fridge, kitchen sink, toaster, or whatever. Dowse further afield to target a church, school, public house, monument or nearby villages. Now dowse for an important invisible target – geographical north. Check the rod's final alignment with a compass, or via the Great Bear constellation and the north star. You will never again need a compass for guidance. Do this exercise many times until you have complete confidence in your ability.

One night our cat, Molly, was outside the house, so I decided to dowse for her. The rod turned to a specific direction but then began to move slowly to the left. After the rod had moved through an angle of around 90 degrees, I went to the window. There, in the moonlight, Molly was sauntering slowly across the lawn.

TRACKING

One can practise following or tracking underground utilities such as water and gas pipes, telecommunication cabling ducts, water drains and sewer pipes. Telecommunication cabling ducts are excellent for initial practice since metal or stone covers conceal the underground servicing pits. Start at one of these pit covers and with a single rod in 'search' align with the direction of the ducting which passes centrally through the service pit. Now 'tune in' to the route of the ducting around bends, uphill or downhill. Confirmation that you are 'on the target' appears when you cross, centrally, over the covers.

The water branch pipe to your home leads to the water mains pipe and is easily found by the water stopcock. You can, likewise, track the water mains: by 'tuning in' to branch pipes with two rods, one rod will turn by 90° to indicate any other branch pipes on the route. The other rod will remain aligned along the direction of the water mains. Should you inadvertently stray from the correct route the rod(s) will point in the direction you must take to stay on course.

Before attempting exercises on tracking utilities, try tracking, say, a path edge, or a lawn edge. At times stray from the route and note how the rods' correction factor points you to the target. The same tracking technique is used for following earth energy flows such as the earth's geodetic energy system and the twin earth energy currents – the 'Michael' and 'Mary' currents. These will be discussed later. I normally 'track' using a single rod.

REMANENCE TRACKING

One of the most intriguing aspects about objects is that when they are moved they leave behind a three-dimensional, etheric ghost of their past presence and this can be readily detected with a single rod in 'search'. Standing stones that have been toppled, or completely removed, leave behind their distinctive 'remanence' trace. At Avebury henge, in Wiltshire, the ditched and banked henge once contained a huge circle of 100 stones in which stood two other stone circles – large by any standard in Europe. At the centre of the southern circle stood a large stone, which dominated the entire complex, and it was known as the 'Obelisk'. A large pyramidal, concrete marker now occupies the Obelisk's position. Here one can experience the powerful remanence of the Obelisk stone. With a single rod in 'search' make a dowsing pass, from any direction, towards the marker, using your accuracy reference. As the reference coincides with the remanence of the outer skin of the missing Obelisk, the rod will zap into 'found'. It's as if you have encountered the stone itself, so powerful is the reaction.

If you wish to delineate the shape of the stone at rod height, use stick markers or small stones. Approach the concrete marker from different directions and each time the rod reacts to 'found' place a marker directly beneath your accuracy reference. The more dowsing passes you make, the more accurate will be the stone's cross-sectional plan. This exercise can, of course, be undertaken at any stone circle with missing stones.

PRACTICE

Try an experiment with an electric torch. Flash the torch beam on to a wall for a second (or less). The torch beam is simply a stream of wave-particles known as photons and each photon in its journey through space leaves its own remanence trail. Now walk at right angles to the vanished beam with a rod in 'search' and detect the beam's remanence.

People and animals also leave these trails and, because of this, they can be tracked easily. Try an initial experiment with a friend on a stretch of open ground. Ask the friend to start off from a certain point and to walk undulatingly around the space, forming loops, figures of eight or triangles along the way. At the starting point cross the friend's path in order to detect the remanence trail then align along it with a single rod in search. Follow the rod's directional guidance and it will take you along your friend's erratic route, geometries and all. Although your friend was visible en route, this initial exercise will give you confidence for another exercise. This time, ask your friend to take a five-minute walk, leaving by, say, the front door and returning by the back door. Now, using a single rod in 'search' make a pass along the front door to pick up the friend's trail and this will determine if the friend turned left or right at the door. Align along the trail and follow the rod's directional guidance and you will track your friend's trail. When you return you can describe the precise details of the walk.

HEED A CAVEAT

I once did this exercise with an old friend who took a 30-minute stroll around the village. I had told him to rest after 30 minutes and I would catch up with him. Eventually the rod took me to a public house but there was no sign of my friend. The bar was a friendly place with a log fire and, as the day was cold, I drank a pint of ale by the fire's warmth. When I eventually returned home there was no sign of my friend but he returned after an hour or so. I had completely failed to find him. But why? We had done this exercise several times before. The failure taught me an important lesson. My friend had been to my house scores of times and had, invariably, walked around the village and had, as a consequence, left many trails along the garden path. I had detected a remanence trail but it wasn't the last remanence trail! These trails persist, possibly indefinitely and, therefore, when tracking a person one should 'tune in' to the person's last remanence trail to the exclusion of all others.

PENDULUM DOWSING

A pendulum can be programmed to give yes/no responses in information dowsing. One method of achieving this is to sit on a chair in an upright position and relax. Hold the pendulum cord at a length that 'feels' right for you. This could be two, three, four or five inches (5, 7.5, 10 or 12.5 cm). Position the pendulum bob so that it is around an inch (2.5 cm) or so above the right kneecap which is a minor 'chakra' region. Now set the pendulum bob in a 'search' swing, that is to say a forward and backward linear oscillation with a swing length of around 3 to 4 inches (7.5 to 10 cm). Now give the quiet command 'show me a "yes" response'. The search swing may continue for a short period and then the bob will produce a 'yes' response. For me the 'yes' response is a clockwise swing. The 'no' response can be found by repeating the procedure over the left kneecap and is, for me, a counter-clockwise swing.

Some of my students have yes/no responses which are opposite to mine and some have responses which are 45° linear swings to the right and to the left; one had a counter-clockwise swing for a 'yes' and an angular linear swing to the left for a 'no'.

You will have your own personal responses and this exercise will establish them. Whatever they are, they will remain with you for life but, remember, before you commence information dowsing tasks, always take a few seconds to check that they are the same as they do alter from time to time – for several hours, perhaps, or even a day or so.

PRACTICE

You can begin information dowsing by repeating the earlier commodity exercise with the L-rod. As information dowsing is an infinite subject, I leave it to your imagination for further exercises.

THE CORRECT CORD LENGTH

Now that you have a 'yes' and 'no' response, you can determine the best cord length for your most successful dowsing. Hold the cord an inch (2.5 cm) from the bob and put it into a linear backward and forward 'search' swing. Now ask the question 'Is this cord length correct for me?' The answer will be 'no'. Now lengthen the cord by about one quarter of an inch (5 mm) and repeat the question at intervals whilst lengthening the cord. When the correct length is reached for your own personal frequency level, the response will be 'yes'.

Now tie a knot at that length. Always dowse with that specific length of cord.

PENDULUM DIRECTIONAL DOWSING

A pendulum will also establish directions. Hold a pendulum so that the bob hangs motionless and then give the command 'Show me geographic north'. The bob will slowly build up its momentum into a linear swing in the direction of north. You will feel the 'pull' towards this cardinal point. Now, in your lounge, repeat the 'show me' exercise to identify objects in the room.

MAP DOWSING

You can dowse a map for virtually anything using a pendulum. Professional dowsing prospectors invariably map dowse for the commodities they seek prior to dowsing a site.

To find a target on a map hold a motionless pendulum bob over the edge of the map at any selected point. Now give the command 'show me the direction of "X".' The pendulum will build up its momentum in a linear swing indicating the target's direction. Note the swing direction closely or, better still, mark the swing direction with a pencil and ruler, drawing the line right across the map. Now select another point on the map's edge and repeat the command. The pendulum will then trace out another linear swing. Draw the line, as before, and the target will be at the intersection of the two lines. This is a two-point fix.

FINDING LOST OBJECTS

You may wish, at times, to find a lost object in your house, in which case draw a plan of the rooms of your house, having first established by information dowsing that the object is upstairs, or downstairs, should you live in a storied house. Then dowse the map, room by room, asking the question 'Is the object in this room?' When you get a 'yes' response you have identified the room associated with the object. Next divide the room plan into four areas and dowse each area to find the location in the room of the object. Now go to that section of the room and look for it.

THE NEED TO KNOW

Major-General J Scott Elliot, a past President of the British Society of Dowsers, mentions in his book *Dowsing – One Man's Way* that dowsing works best 'when there is a need to know'. From my own experience I agree with him as do several other dowsing colleagues. Party tricks, where there isn't a real need to know, tend to go awry and I never indulge in these. As I see it, if a dowser tries such party tricks he, or she, is engaged in an egotistical exercise.

How map dowsing works is an inexplicable enigma. One is detecting invisible, yet tangible, things such as electromagnetic radiations, magnetic fields, radioactivity, electrostatic fields, etc in practical dowsing. We know the radiations exist and can attune to them. In map dowsing, however, we are absent from the locations of our enquiries and are pendulum dowsing a sheet made from paper pulp and coloured inks. Yuri Geller is one of the best exponents of map dowsing for all types of minerals, oil and gas although he is mainly known for his esoteric acts of spoon bending and stopping or starting clocks. Many large industrial corporations have employed Yuri Geller. Unlike the many 'tunnel-visioned' scientists who either ignore dowsing or do not believe in its scope, the industrial corporations have no 'hang-ups' about dowsing, as they get results.

PRACTICE

For pendulum dowsing practice use an ordnance survey map and ask a friend to study the map and name a location for you to detect, such as a farm-house, water works, a long barrow or whatever, then find the place with two-point fixes.

QUO VADIS?

Where do we go from here? As in all skills practice makes perfect so practise dowsing often and your sensitivity, or psi-factor, will improve significantly. Try to establish what I call your 'dowsing credibility factor' with both rods and pendulum. In other words, on a percentage scale, what is your dowsing credibility? If it is, for example, 50 per cent then why bother with dowsing tools? You may as well simply flip a coin.

In my early dowsing days I recorded my successes and failures over 100 dowsing passes where the results were verifiable. I found that my credibility factor was 70 per cent. After another

month of daily practice I made a second record of 100 dowsing passes but this time I analyzed every failure more closely. The result this time was 85 per cent. In-depth failure analysis was important and I found many reasons for the errors.

They were due, for example, to:

- Forgetting to use my accuracy reference. A few inches deviation from a target I considered as a failure even though I may have made a dowsing pass of 100 paces to arrive at a 'found' reaction!
- Not preparing adequately for the task and approaching it in a blasé manner.
- Poor visualization and letting the mind wander.
- Dowsing fatigue – at times I had dowsed for hours without rest.
- 'Frame of mind' disturbances by passing cars and peoples' voices. I had not re-established my frame of mind. My relaxed concentration had been broken.
- Dowsing too quickly and not allowing the dowsing rod to overcome its inertia.
- The cardinal sin of auto-suggestion.

In a further 100 dowsing passes my credibility factor soared to 97 per cent as I eliminated the causes of errors.

Use dowsing as a way of life rather than an interesting hobby. Information dowsing can be used, for example, to make a variety of decisions in business or daily life. You may be planning a journey by car and there are three possible routes. Dowse the one take that will be the least trouble with delays arising from congested traffic, road works, etc. You have an air journey to make with several flights available to take on the day. Dowse to find the flight which will be devoid of delays due to technical troubles, or whatever.

Dowse for the best period to take a vacation for weather conditions and, if there is a choice of hotels, dowse for the one that will be best for you in comfort, cuisine and service standards.

In a business you may have the choice of a number of suppliers of, say, electrical components. Dowse for the supplier that will best meet your requirements in delivery promises, quality and reliability. One can begin to see the scope of dowsing as a way of life. The only limit is the imagination.

Dowsers are becoming increasingly popular for finding a variety of artefacts. To find, say, a Roman coin in a field with the use of a metal detector, one has to scan up and down the field in a thorough survey and this takes time. In dowsing, one hasn't to do this. Firstly, by 'information dowsing', establish if there are coins buried in the field. If the answer is 'no', waste no more time. Metal detector exponents have to establish this the hard way. If the answer is 'yes', use the directional finding technique with a single rod in 'search' and give the command 'Show me the direction of the nearest Roman coin.' When the rod swivels to rest follow its direction until it swings into the 'found' position. The coin is here. If more coins are in the field, repeat the directional dowsing procedure.

Dowsing for earth and aerial energies is a fascinating subject which I discovered was my main forté, especially at prehistoric monuments such as stone circles, medieval churches and cathedrals whose foundation plans incorporate the subtle earth energy flows and geometric patterns. These subjects can widen your dowsing horizons considerably as the ancient Greek temples have been geomantically designed on the same earth energy principles. If you spend a vacation in Greece, take the dowsing rods and pendulum with you. Visit the Parthenon and other temples on the mainland and the Greek islands.

Now we will widen our dowsing experiences in the remaining chapters and engage in identifying diverse dowsing phenomena.

EARTH ENERGIES

Dowsing for earth energies is a fascinating dimension in which we find exotic patterns and mystifying geometries interlacing the surface of the planet. These may take the form of spectacular spirals, global energy grids and great geomantic rivers of earth energies. In the 1940s the late Guy Underwood discovered a complex system of earth energies which he called 'the geodetic system'. The system comprises distinctive energy flows, great haloes, arc clusters, geospirals and necklaces. However, as space does not allow for descriptions of all the geodetic elements, we will concentrate on just one particular geodetic geometry – the geospiral (earth spiral). Readers wishing to explore further elements in the geodetic system should read Guy's book *The Pattern of the Past*, which is available in public libraries. In my books *Dowsing With a Difference* and *A New View of Stonehenge* the geodetic system is covered in detail, including many of Guy Underwood's energy surveys. Several of them were unpublished and are revealed for the first time.

Geospirals are associated with 'blind springs' (also called 'water domes' in America). They appear as energetic, harmonic surface patterns in the earth.

BLIND SPRINGS

A blind spring is water that is produced chemically deep within the earth. Under high pressure, the water is forced towards the earth's surface through vertical geological faults and may break through as a spring. However, if the water meets an impenetrable rock strata it 'domes' and under the sustained pressure it then escapes through every available rock fissure at all levels and so produces underground streams.

THE GEOSPIRAL

A geospiral is a geometrically-perfect spiral with coils in multiples of seven: 3½, 7, 14, 21, 28, 35, 42 and 49. In the neolithic and bronze ages blind springs appear to have been revered as sacred space. Guy Underwood found that at megalithic sites the important features were invariably located over these springs. At Stonehenge, for example, the Altar Stone is set over a 7-coil spiral and the Heel Stone is set over a 49-coil spiral.

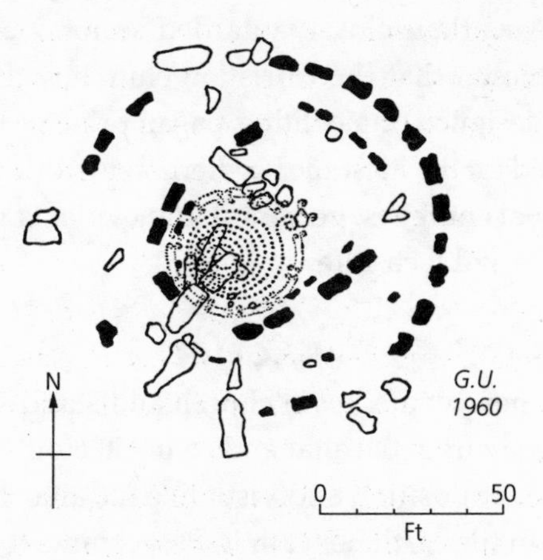

The seven-coil spiral below the Altar Stone at Stonehenge

Geospirals are to be found at the centres of stone circles, at long barrows, dolmen constructs, round barrows and man-made hills. Solitary standing stones mark blind springs. Such stones did not mark the location as a potential water supply, since in the neolithic and bronze ages the technology for drilling through rock strata did not exist. The stone marked sacred space. In over 20 years of research Guy Underwood found that every round barrow was located over a blind spring. Clearly, the men of prehistory could detect the geospirals by divination. Geospiral cave carvings 30,000 years old are found in Europe and also in Australian aboriginal art and North American Indian art, implying knowledge of geospirals was archetypal.

This obsession with water in the ancient religions has parallels in modern religions. Consider the holy Ganges and the sacred lake Titicaca, holy wells and springs and the use in rituals of holy water.

The knowledge of the geodetic system was passed down through the neolithic, bronze and iron ages and the final guardians of this were the medieval European masonic brotherhood. This was their closely guarded secret. Had the church hierarchy known that the Christian churches and cathedrals were being designed on neolithic, pagan principles, they would have rounded on the masonic brotherhood with a vengeance.

At medieval churches, geospirals are evident at altars, fonts, towers, spires and lych gates.

PRACTICE

- Go to a nearby medieval church and stand some 30 to 40 paces away from the altar and facing it. Hold a single rod in the 'search' position and visualize the altar's geospiral of energy in the earth beneath it. Programme the rod to react when your accuracy indicator (such as the thumb tip) is coincident with each coil of the spiral. Now make a slow, straight dowsing pass towards the altar. Most altar geospirals have seven coils so you are likely to obtain seven distinct rod reactions. Altar geospirals vary from around ten to twenty paces in radius. Reset the rod to 'search' after each reaction.

- Now check the church font for its geospiral and also the spire or tower. If the church has a lych gate check this location for a geospiral. Check also burial round barrows and long barrows, solitary standing stones and the centres of stone circles for geospirals. See 'Places of Interest' at the end of the book for some suggested locations.
- American readers should check Indian sacred sites for geospirals.

EARTH ENERGY RIVERS

> There are in the earth's crust two different, shall I say magnetic currents, the one male, the other female, the one positive, the other negative.
>
> FROM *FENG-SHUI, THE SCIENCE OF SACRED LANDSCAPES IN ANCIENT CHINA,*
> EJ EITEL (1873)

In 1985 Hamish Miller and Paul Broadhurst discovered two great geomantic rivers of earth energies coursing for 300 miles across southern England from Land's End to Hopton on the Norfolk coast, which they dubbed Michael (yang) and Mary (yin). Along the undulations of these intertwining energy rivers were over 300 sacred sites and medieval churches aligned with high accuracy along the currents. They had, in effect, found the earth's 'dragon lines' so highly revered by the ancient Chinese feng-shui geomancers.

FENG-SHUI AT AVEBURY

In the neolithic ritual landscape of Avebury, feng-shui is vividly demonstrated by both the megalithic and medieval masons. On their arrival in the region, the twin earth currents engage in a sinuous, energetic ballet. This earth ballet was recognized by the neolithic builders and we see how they integrated these coursings into the main features they had created on this sacred landscape.

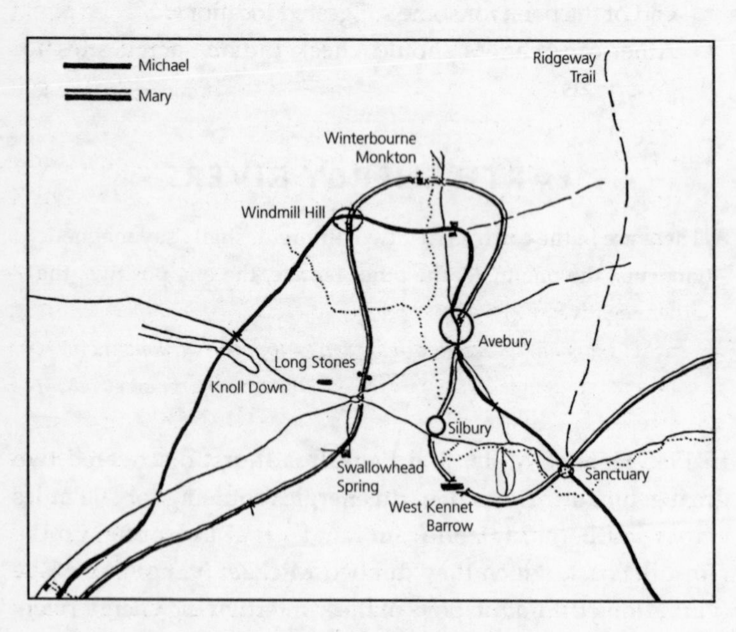

Michael and Mary currents at Avebury

Pendragon Press, Launceston, Cornwall can provide ordnance survey maps covering the counties through which the twin currents course, duly marked with their meanderings. Now, for practice, dowse the twin currents in the Avebury region.

Remember to visualize Michael as a scintillating river of silver energy and Mary as a scintillating river of blue energy.

- Dowse for the leading and trailing edges of the currents at the various locations shown in the illustration.
- Dowse for Mary coursing alone through the West Kennet long barrow and setting the axis and width of the church at Winterbourne Monkton, a village close to Avebury. (Check the church geospirals at the altar and font.)
- Check the crossing points of the currents at the Sanctuary and on Windmill Hill. A tumulus marks the crossing point on Windmill Hill.
- At the Sanctuary, Michael courses in from the west and oblong concrete blocks mark the location of the Kennet Avenue stones. These set Michael's width. So, dowse beteen these two rows of blocks for Michael's leading and trailing edges. Mary courses across the Sanctuary in a north-easterly direction passing through the cluster of round barrows in the field just by the ridgeway trail. Position yourself some fifteen paces to the south-west of the Sanctuary entrance gate. You are now standing at the centre of the Mary current. Now make a dowsing pass to your left to find one edge of the current. Then from the same central position make another dowsing pass to your right to find the other edge. You will note that, at this site, Mary is wider than Michael.
- At the tumulus on Windmill Hill, make a 360-degree dowsing pass around the mound, 'tuning in' to Michael to

find its edges. Now repeat the dowsing pass but 'tune in' to Mary.

- At the Cove feature on the northern circle, check for the Mary current flowing from the Cove to target the solitary nearby megalith, which is a survivor of the northern stone circle.

THE APOLLO AND ATHENA CURRENTS

Whilst dowsing for the Michael and Mary earth energy currents on Saint Michael's Mount, Hamish Miller and Paul Broadhurst became aware of two other major earth energy currents, but with different energy signatures.

Through the work of the brothers – Jean and Lucien Richer – Hamish and Paul realized that these other earth energy currents coursed from the island of Skellig Saint Michael, off the coast of Ireland, to mount Carmel in Israel. Like Michael and Mary, these currents had yang and yin characteristics and were dubbed Apollo and Athena.

Along their 2,500-mile meandering, there are an astonishing number of sanctuaries across Europe, including Lindos, Delos, Athens, Delphi, Kerkyra (Corfu), Mount Gargano, Perugin, Sacra Di San Michele, Bourses, Mont Saint Michel, Saint Michael's mount and Skellig Saint Michael.

Prior to setting off on this 2,500-mile dowsing odyssey, Hamish found that the weaving Apollo and Athena lines passed through holy wells, churches and hill forts in Cornwall.

Hamish Miller and his partner, Ba Russell, have been tracking Apollo and Athena for the past 4 years and their findings will be published in a forthcoming book.

THE GLOBAL ENERGY GRIDS

There are two global grids which cover the planet from pole to pole like gigantic fishnets of standing wave energy. The first global grid was discovered by Dr Manfred Curry and the second global grid by Dr Ernst Hartmann.

THE FIRST GLOBAL GRID

This grid is also known as 'the Curry global net' and is aligned northwest–southeast.

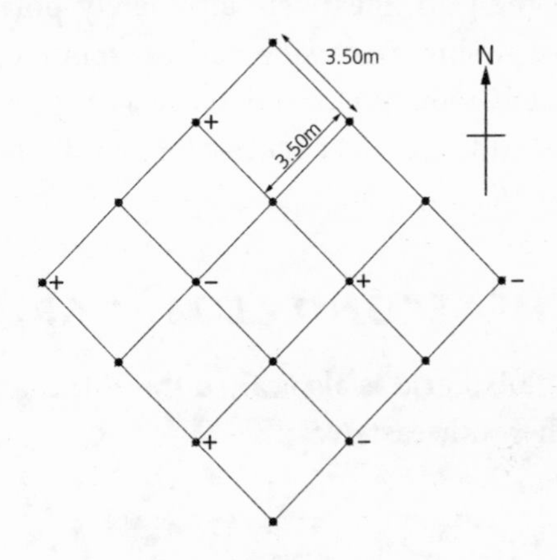

The Curry Global Net. The Curry net diagram of Ilse Pope. Reproduced by kind permission of the British Society of Dowsers.

As we shall see later, the crossing points of this grid can be adverse to health with long-term exposure to them. It is believed that the grid is terrestrial in origin and caused by the core magma radiations of the earth, its rotation and magnetic field.

- To detect the grid, align to the northwest with a single rod in 'search' and visualize the grid lines as silver walls of standing energy. Now make a slow, straight dowsing pass. When your accuracy indicator aligns with the first grid line, the rod will react to 'found'. Return to 'search' and a reaction will occur at the next line. The reactions in the dowsing pass will be in 3.5 metre intervals – the dimensions of the grid.
- Now make a similar dowsing pass at right angles to the first pass to detect the other grid lines. Again, the reactions will be 3.5 metres apart.
- We saw the grid lines were alternately polarized. Make another dowsing pass to the northwest but 'tune in' to the positive lines only and the rod will react at 7-metre intervals.
- Likewise, tune into the negative lines and establish them 7 metres apart.

THE SECOND GLOBAL GRID

The second global grid is also called the Hartmann net and is aligned north–south, east–west.

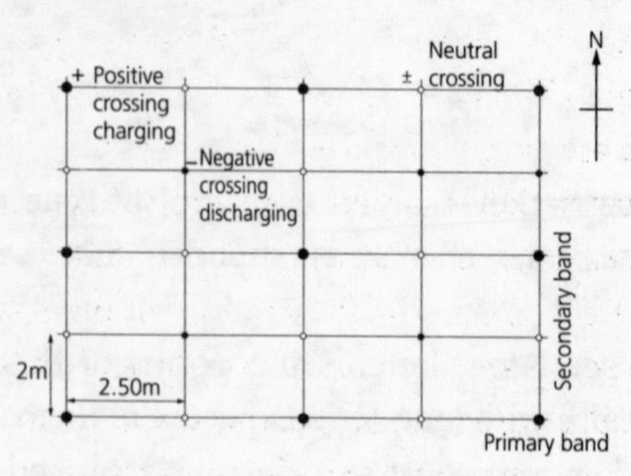

The Hartmann net. The Hartmann net diagram of Ilse Pope. Reproduced by kind permission of the British Society of Dowsers.

This grid is thought to be cosmic in origin and related to the two Van-Allen belts of high intensity particle radiations at 16,000 km and 24,000 km.

The Hartmann net is also polarized alternately but has phase changes every 6 hours at sunrise, noon, sunset and midnight. The radiation intensity of the grid varies with the full moon and changing weather fronts.

PRACTICE

Confirm the grid lines and their polarities to the north–south and east–west, as for the Curry grid.

TRACK LINES

A 'track line' is a form of energy flow comprising 6 parallel hair-lines of no appreciable width and is one of three types of energy flow in the geodetic system of earth energies. In making a dowsing pass across a track line, 6 dowsing reactions will be obtained. The overall width of a track line is around 6 to 10 feet (18 to 30 m).

Track lines follow ancient trails such as the Ridgeway trail in southern England and the Icknield way which runs from Hertfordshire to join the Ridgeway. They also follow old country lanes and aboriginal trails in Australia and North America. In South America they run with Inca roads.

Migrating caribou and wildebeest follow track lines, as do domestic cattle. A cattle trail in a field will invariably follow a track line. Here we are faced with an enigma. Did the track lines exist in the earth from time immemorial and people instinctively followed them, or did the passing of thousands of people down a trailway create the six energy lines?

PRACTICE

- Find track lines on ancient trails, old country roads or medieval church pathways. With a single rod in 'search', make a straight dowsing pass across the selected target to obtain the 6 rod reactions.
- Find a track line on an old, undulating road and with two rods in 'search' track the line. A track line can create another track line which may deviate from the route along a road to the gate of a field. One rod will then remain in forward 'search' whilst the other will point either left or right indicating the line deviation.
- Now follow the deviating track line to see if it coincides with hoof-marked trails across the field.

FORM ENERGY

Circles create circular, polarized, energetic bands in a phenomenon known as 'form energy'. This is shown in the Rollright Ring illustration.

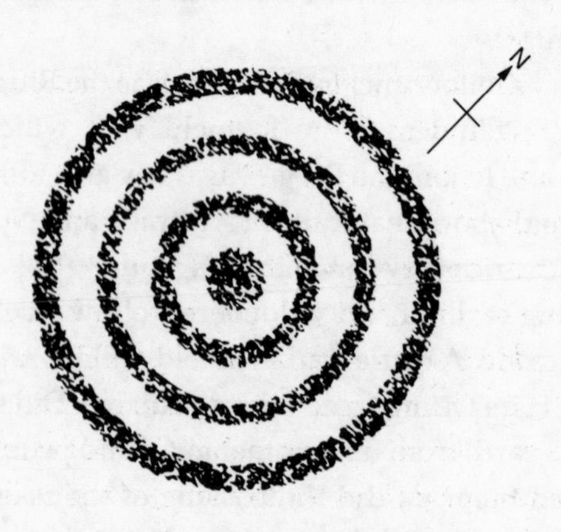

The Rollright Ring

The bands are alternately polarized, the black bands being positive and the band spacings between them negative. The bands extend outside the circle and spread across the countryside, gradually weakening in strength with distance from the circle.

PRACTICE

- Stand at the circumference of any stone circle with a single rod in 'search' and visualize the polarized bands. Now make a straight, slow dowsing pass to the centre. As your accuracy indicator aligns with the first band the rod will swing to 'found' and this indicates 'positive'. Keep the rod in the 'found' position and at the next band the rod will swing to 'search' indicating a negative band. Continue in this dowsing mode to the centre.
- Now dowse for the bands outside the circle, using the same technique.

Form energy and the first and second global grids have confused many dowsers who have written articles on dowsing crop pictograms.

One wrote 'The crop circle must be genuine because in and around it are concentric, polarized bands'. *All* crop circles, whether genuine or hoaxed, will generate this energy phenomenon and so the comment is invalid and confuses the issue. A circle drawn on a sheet of plain paper will, likewise, generate the form energy bands.

Another dowser wrote that 'the crop circle was unusual and must be the real thing since it contained a grid of energy lines'. He must have picked up either the Curry or Hartmann global grids, as these grids cover the planet from pole to pole. The grids appear everywhere, including hoaxed crop circles. Such flights of fanciful nonsense confuse people and do the dowsing discipline no good.

METEOROLOGICAL EFFECTS ON DOWSING REACTION FIELDS

In 1935, JC Maby and TB Franklin researched the relationship between changes in dowsing reactions and the magnetic field strength over an underground stream under different weather conditions. The results revealed a positive correlation between climate conditions and magnetic field strength variations and dowsing reactions.

The changes in magnetic strength and dowsing reactions proved to be almost perfectly in phase with each other in their graphed undulations. The weather changes preceded them by a few hours.

The results were recorded in their book *The Physics of the Divining Rod* (Bell, 1939). The two authors were electrical engineers and, through their research, became part of the British Society of Dowser's committee investigating dowsing and dowsing reactions. The correlations are shown below.

Weather Conditions	Dowsing Reactions	Magnetic Field Strengths
Wet	Low	Low
Fine and frosty	High (peak)	High (peak)
Foggy	Low	Low
Cold with snow	Low	Low
Fine and warm	High (peak)	High (peak)
Gales with rain	Low	Low
Fine and settled	High (peak)	High (peak)

The results were checked over a ten-day period in December and indicate the highly variable climatic changes in the south-west of England in December.

The results suggest that both the dowsing field and the dowsing reactions vary with the weather at this location. Dr J Havelock Fidler, whose research we will discuss later, checked what he called his psi-factor, or dowsing sensitivity, over a complete lunar phase and found it at its peak level at 4pm on the day of the full moon. I do not know how he measured his sensitivity. Experiments on dowsing sensitivity were undertaken by Dr Z Harvalik in America. Dowsers were requested to dowse an electric wire with a few milli-amperes of current passing through it. The current produces an electromagnetic field around the wire. The current was gradually reduced and so the electromagnetic field became weaker. At various minute current levels the field was not detected by some dowsers.

AERIAL ENERGY DOWSING

LEY LINES

In 1925 Alfred Watkins published his book *The Old Straight Track*, which was revolutionary in revealing that Britain was interlaced with laser-like lines which he called 'ley lines'.

At around the same time, in Germany, Wilhelm Teudt was researching linearities, and he reached the same conclusions as Alfred Watkins. Teudt called his linearities 'heilige linien', or 'holy lines'.

This remarkable linear engineering is prehistoric in origin and is topographically marked by standing stones, stone circles, long barrows, round barrows, moated mounds, dolmen chambers and stone cairns. This prehistoric obsession with linearity was archetypal, as ley lines appear on all continents.

AERIAL LEY ENERGY

Over the past 50 years or so, various dowsers have reported that an aerial-type energy was passing between standing stones on ley lines. This remained nothing more than a curiosity until a retired scientist, Dr J Havelock Fidler, decided to research both the nature and origin of this energy.

Dr Fidler had read *The Power of the Pendulum* by Tom Lethbridge, which revealed that if a male held a pebble, then a pendulum held over it would rotate clockwise. If a female held a pebble, then the pendulum held over it would rotate counter-clockwise. It would appear that the crystal lattice structure of the pebble 'memorized' the bionic field of the person holding it. The bionic memory was, however, transient and the pebble reverted to neutral within 24 hours.

A pendulum held over the head of a male will swing clockwise, and over the head of a female it will swing counter-clockwise, recording the bionic fields.

BIONIC CHARGING

Dr Fidler confirmed this transient bionic charging phenomenon, but found that if a pebble experienced a dynamic shock when it was held, then the bionic charge was 'locked in' – probably for all time. A light hammer blow would induce a small bionic charge but a heavy blow would induce a much higher charge. The charging level was directly in proportion to the degree of hammering. He found that if a stone was placed on a fire, the bionic charge was permanently locked into it through thermal shock. He devised an instrument – a gyrometer – to record the charging levels in units which he called 'petrons'. This was a light source shining onto a horizontal graded scale. If a pebble is placed between the light source and the scale and dowsed with a pendulum, the gyrating cord appears on the scale as a shadow and records in notional numbers the petron charge levels.

LITHON POWER

Dr Fidler also found that if a stone acquired a petron charge, it had a power which he calculated in units of 'lithons'. This

lithon power calculation was simple: lithon power = petron charge level × the mass of the stone. So, for a given charge of, say, 50 petrons, a large stone would have a greater lithon power than a smaller stone.

PRACTICE

Ask a male and a female to hold some stones. Then, by pendulum dowsing, confirm the findings of Tom Lethbridge. Check the stones after 24 hours for the absence of charges.

LEY LINE ENERGY

In acquiring petron charges and lithon powers, stones have the ability to transmit to other stones an aerial-type energy. Dr Fidler made a miniature ley line with pebbles and on dowsing between the pebbles his pendulum rotated rapidly in response to the aerial energy passing down the line.

He also noted that the aerial energy was not confined to the line. The end pebbles transmitted the energy out into his laboratory as if seeking other stones to latch onto.

PRACTICE

Make a miniature ley line with charged stones and confirm Dr Fidler's findings. Check that the end pebbles or stones transmit the energy outside the miniature ley. Use a pendulum with the bob positioned about half an inch (1 cm) over the ground, or table.

FREQUENCY AND WAVELENGTHS

In a series of elegant experiments Dr Fidler found the frequency and wavelength of the energy and also that the energy beam was in the nature of a triad, ie three parallel hairlines. The area where he lived near Loch Shieldaig, Scotland, was rich in standing stones and these he mapped out.

He discovered that each stone was transmitting aerial energies to the other stones in the region. Some stones had as many as seven aerial beams passing through them and these he called 'beacon' stones. The beams had the same wavelengths and frequencies as his laboratory ley lines, and were 'triads' comprising three energetic hairlines. He named an aerial beam triad a 'petrostat'.

But if this energy was bionically induced in the standing stones, how could it be caused? He noted that many of the stones had been sculpted into shape by the neolithic masons. The stones must have been struck thousands of times with axes and mauls so that each dynamic shock locked the bionic fields of the masons into the crystal lattice structures of the stones for all time.

Evidently, this was the charging mechanism and because of the huge mass of the stones, their lithon powers were enormous.

The five great lintelled pairs of stones which dominated Stonehenge's inner sanctum must have been struck millions of times as they were sculpted from the rough into lozenge-shaped cross sections by gangs of masons, resulting in high bionic charging. Due to their huge masses, they must have the greatest lithon power of any other stones. The uprights of these stones varied in height between 20 and 24 feet (60 and 72 m) and in weight between 45 and 50 tons.

In his research, Dr Fidler found that quartz crystals absorbed the aerial energy of a standing stone at source, and so inhibited the transmission. The weight of crystals to inhibit beaming was directly related to the mass of the stone. He produced a chart showing the amount of crystal weight needed to inhibit transmissions in stones of different tonnage. These findings were revealed in his book *Ley Lines* (Thorsons). For the first time here was a coherent ley line theory confirming the associated aerial-type energy and its nature.

THE LABYRINTH COIL

Aerial energy associated with standing stones is not acceptable to the body scientific. In science one must be able to measure or weigh and to replicate results in experiments. If a phenomenon cannot be detected, then it does not exist.

A friend of mine, Bob Sephton, is a retired electrical engineer and an experienced dowser with a highly questing mind. He experimented with different types of copper coils wired to an oscilloscope, an instrument for showing energy variations on a small screen. A coil based on the labyrinth in Chartres cathedral was placed at the end of a long pole and wired to the oscilloscope. The objective was to detect aerial ley energy. He picked two standing stones, which he had dowsed for aerial ley energy. The idea of the pole was to eliminate from the experiment any body radiations, including Burr's L-field (life field) which can be detected with electronic instruments.

The oscilloscope remained quiescent until Bob placed the coil within the ley line. The oscilloscope's horizontal line then danced wildly. On removing the coil the oscilloscope line sank back to the horizontal 'no energy' level.

Bob visited Dr Fidler and showed him the method of establishing the existence of a ley energy line. Dr Fidler danced with exuberant joy at this significant breakthrough in ley line detection. The energy was now in the realms of science and could not be denied.

In the following sections practical field work will be discussed so that readers can gain dowsing experience of aerial ley energy.

STONE TRANSMISSION BANDS

A standing stone has a series of nodes, or bands, five in number above ground level. The first is at or near the base of the stone and the rest are at different levels with the fifth band being near the crest. These bands are highly dowsable. (Church buttresses also have these bands).

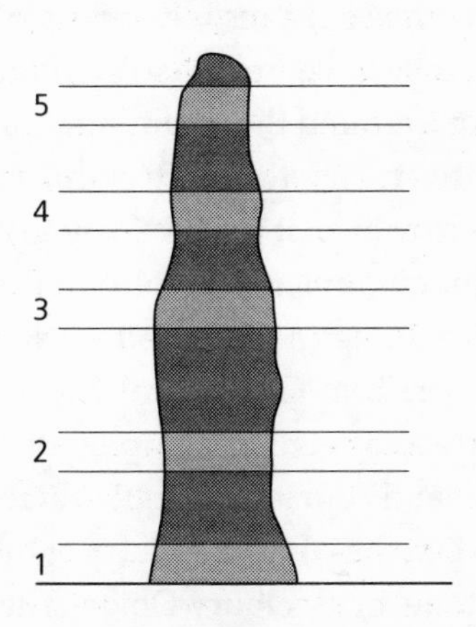

Energy nodes of small and tall megaliths

In the illustration, Band 2 is for aerial transmissions to local stones such as those in a stone circle, whilst band 4 is for longer distance transmissions to other megalithic sites. The purpose of the other bands remains unknown. Smaller stones have only 3 bands.

PRACTICE

Visit a stone circle, a single standing stone or a church buttress to confirm the bands.

Use a single L-rod in the inverted position so that the rod can swing close to the ground. The aim is to find the bottom and top of the first band. Tune in to the first band and raise the rod from ground level, very slowly. At the top and bottom of band 1 the rod will swing. Now put the rod back into 'search' position and raise it slowly up the face of the stone to detect the bottoms and tops of the remaining bands.

ENERGY 'CROSS-TALK'

Every stone in a circle engages with every other stone in energetic frontal cross talk. There is also a cyclotronic spin energy from stone to stone around the circumference of the circle.

In a circle with many stones, it is difficult to unravel the cross-talk skein. However, it is fairly easy to detect the spinning energy around the circumference from stone to stone.

At the Rollright Ring in Oxfordshire, stones 20 and 21 are offset. The dowser, Tom Graves, called this 'the eastern exit gate'. At the gate a tangential component of the spin energy passes through it and courses, laser-like, across the countryside for six miles and latches onto a solitary standing stone known as 'The Hawk Stone' on Spelbury Down. The Hawk Stone is on a ley line known as the Hoare Stone ley line.

PRACTICE

To find the aerial spin energy, use a single rod in 'search' and programme the rod to react when your accuracy indicator coincides with the first hairline of the petrostat. Then, slowly walk between any two stones to get a first reaction. At this point stand still and move the rod very slowly forward to get the second and third reactions, thereby confirming that the energy exists and is triad in nature.

To find in which direction the energy spins, programme a single rod in 'search' to align along the spin direction. Walk between two stones and the rod will align in the spin direction.

CONCENTRIC SHELLS AND CARDINAL RAYS

Standing stones generate spectacular energetic patterns known as concentric shells and cardinal rays. These were deeply researched in the 1930s by JC Maby and TB Franklin. The shells and rays are electromagnetic in nature and rise vertically from the earth. When dowsing these, one walks 'through' the energies rather than 'over' them and so I loosely classify them as aerial energies.

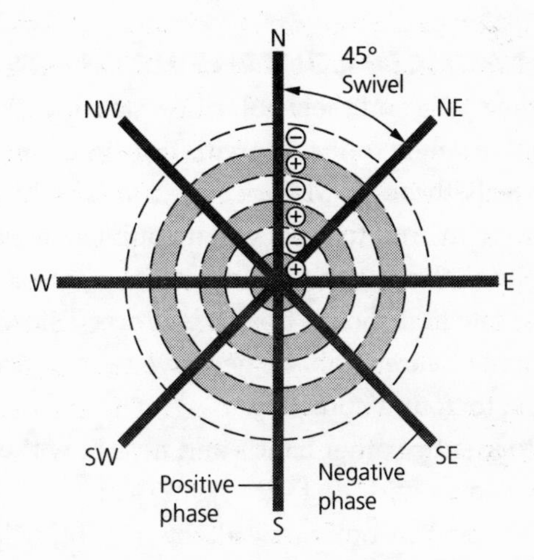

Concentric electromagnetic shells and cardinal rays thrown out by standing stones

Note the shells are alternately charged positive and negative and that the rays target the main compass points. This orientation is known as 'positive' phase and coincides with fine, settled weather. However, if the weather changes to unsettled conditions, then the cardinal rays swivel by 45 degrees to target the intermediate compass points. When this happens, the concentric shells revert from positive to negative and vice-versa. This is known as 'negative' phase.

When the weather changes to fine and settled conditions, the rays swivel back to the main compass points and the shells revert to their original polarities.

These shells and rays are the most spectacular energies associated with standing stones. The energies are powerful and easy to detect. At some stone circles, sightseers who have never dowsed before often try dowsing for the shells and are amazed when they find them.

PRACTICE – CONCENTRIC SHELLS

To identify the shells and their polarities, stand with your back to a stone with a single rod in 'search'. Tune in to the shells you are about to walk through. Make a slow, straight dowsing pass and programme the rod to react when your accuracy indicator aligns with the shells. When the rod reacts to 'found' keep it in that position. The first shell is positive. Proceed slowly and the rod will swing to 'search'. This is negative. At the next shell the rod will swing to 'found', positive.

Carry on to identify other bands and note how the energy of the bands weakens with distance from the stone. Ultimately, this attenuation will become so weak that the rod will not react. The band widths are related to the above ground height of standing stones. A 6-feet (1.8 m) stone will generate 6-feet band widths. This relationship holds for above-ground heights of up to 16 feet (4.8 m). Stones taller than this will generate band widths of 16 feet. In practice, confirm this relationship. The first 'found' reaction should be equal to the stone's height.

PRACTICE — THE CARDINAL RAYS

With a single rod in 'search', make a full 360-degree dowsing pass around the stone. There will be eight dowsing reactions, two for each ray. Remember, if the weather is fine and settled the rays will target the main compass points. As the width of the rays is governed by the outer dimensions of the stone in the direction of either the main or intermediate compass points, they may be unequal in width.

Like the concentric polarized shells, the cardinal ray energies are electromagnetic in nature and rise vertically from the ground. In detecting them you are walking *through* them. The cardinal rays do not have polarities.

LOOSE LEY ENERGIES

During his ley energy researches, Dr J Havelock Fidler noted that trees in the path of aerial ley energies were gnarled, stunted and had unhealthy growths.

In a series of experiments he grew mustard plants from seeds in plant pots. Some of the pots were exposed to aerial ley energy and others were placed away from the energy line. The plants exposed to the energy were badly stunted and deformed whilst the others had normal, healthy growth.

There are 'loose' aerial energies which can pass through houses and can affect the occupants with a variety of illnesses. Loose ley energy lines result from blasting the land to create motorways and other civil engineering projects, thus eliminating standing stones. Down the centuries standing stones have been removed by farmers or smashed for building materials, and so their associated aerial energies become 'loose' and seek other stone targets.

PRACTICE

Dowse around the exterior of your home to detect any aerial energy entering the building. Should you find any, then the following counter-measures can be taken.

As we saw earlier, Dr Fidler found that quartz crystals placed on a stone would block aerial ley energy transmissions. The crystals can also block the arrival of ley energy.

If an aerial ley energy line targets your home, then find its aboveground height. The ley energy is a 'petrostat' comprising three energetic hairlines and so it has a width.

To find the ley energy's height above ground, simply put the rod into 'search' and from ground level slowly raise the rod until you get a 'found' reaction. This is the ley's above-ground height.

To block the energy, place a quartz crystal at the inner hairline height. This will mean erecting a pole-type platform to locate the crystal at the central hairline of the ley energy. The crystal should be approximately two cubic inches (5 cm^3) in size. If you have a garden, place the crystal at the point where the ley enters the garden.

Later we will discuss counter-measures to be taken in homes which contain other geopathic stress zones which are inimical to health. Much research has been done on geopathic stress zones over the past fifty years or so and, as we shall see, Käthe Bachler was a leading researcher in this field.

WATER DIVINING

Over the past few hundred years many celebrated water diviners have emerged. Every village seems to have had its 'village dowser' who, without being taught the skill, could find water supplies instinctively. Such dowsers were, in general, men of few words who would find it difficult to explain their skills. As 'water finding' was a source of income to them, they may have simply been protecting their 'trade secrets'. In America, the water finders are called 'water-witchers'.

In modern times, however, things have changed. Guy Underwood was a man of many talents and, before he concentrated on earth energy dowsing, was a water finder who wrote and lectured on the theory and practice of water finding.

Among the papers I inherited from Guy were his copious notes on water finding which form the basis of this chapter. His questing mind reveals some fascinating concepts associated with underground streams which readers may wish to investigate to widen their dowsing experience.

POSITIVE AND NEGATIVE DOWSERS

An underground stream generates a distinctive surface pattern known as the 'stream band'.

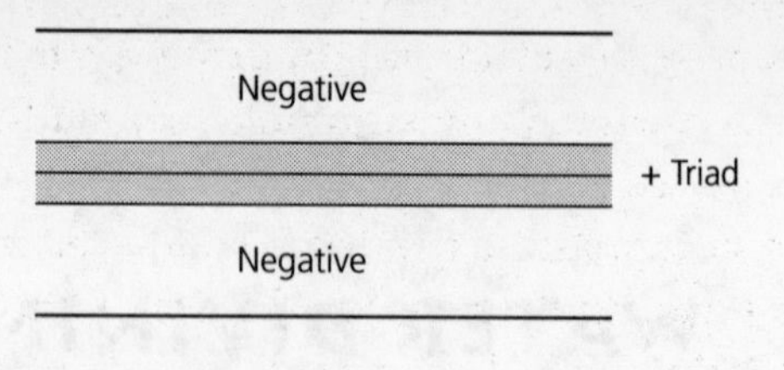

The stream bands

The central triad of lines is positive and to either side are negative zones. Dowsers can be classified as positive or negative according to their reactions to the stream band polarities.

POSITIVE DOWSERS

Positive dowsers are those who have been taught the skill or who have taught themselves from books. On crossing the stream band at right angles they will get three rod reactions at the triad. The negative zones have no influence on them.

NEGATIVE DOWSERS

Negative dowsers are, in general, those instinctive dowsers who can find water without having been taught the skill. They often use the time-honoured Y-rod.

When a negative dowser enters a negative zone, the tip of the Y-rod begins to rise under tension. This rising tension increases as the centre of the stream is approached. On reaching the centre, the rod flops, inertly. Such dowsers do not react to the triad.

PRACTICE

It is not necessary to find an underground stream to practise on the stream band. Running along the lane past my house is a surface stream crossed at intervals by driveways to houses. At such points the stream is 'underground'. My students practise at these locations.

Find a surface stream that has been covered in any way, be it by driveways, bridle paths or whatever. With a single rod in 'search' make a slow dowsing pass over the stream and detect the three lines of the positive triad. As you are learning your dowsing skills from a book, you will be a positive dowser reacting to the positive triad. It is unlikely that any reader will react to the negative zones.

THE PARALLELS

An underground stream throws out to either side of the positive triad a series of equally-spaced triads known as the parallels. The distance from the centre of the stream to the first parallel is equal to the underground depth of the stream. This is known as the Bishop's depthing method (wrongly attributed to the Bishop of Grenoble!).

This depthing method was actually described in the book *La Verge de Jacob*, published in the 17th century.

PRACTICE

Make a dowsing pass from the centre of the stream to either side to detect the inner parallels. Check that the distances from the centre to the inner parallels are equal to the depth of the stream – that is from, say, the driveway to the stream's surface.

THE HARMONICS

Between each set of parallels there exists a series of what Guy called harmonic lines or 'H-bands' which run straight, or undulatingly, with the parallels. He defined them as H1, H2, and H3 bands as shown in the illustration.

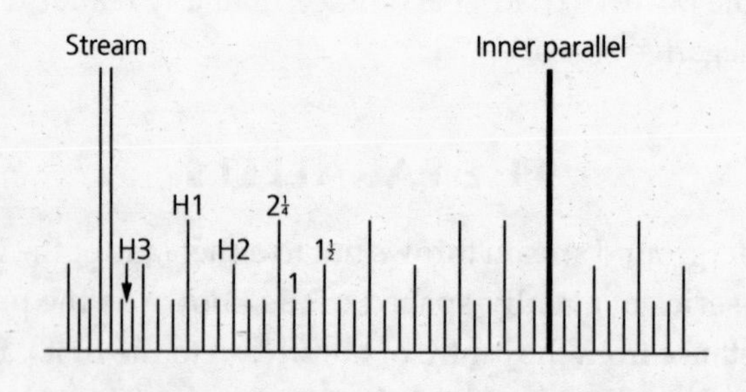

The harmonic lines

Their relative reaction strengths are H1 = 2.25; H2 = 1.50; and H3 = 1. Although knowledge of the harmonic bands will not assist in the least in finding underground water, the phenomenon is interesting in that a stream can generate such energies between the parallel lines of influence.

PRACTICE

Here is another opportunity to practise fine dowsing in establishing the H-bands. Use a single rod in 'search'.

THE PARALLEL CONFUSION

When two or more streams run parallel with each other an amateur dowser can be confused by coincidental sets of parallels. The illustration shows the ground plan of two streams 'A' and 'B' at 50 and 60 feet (15 and 18 m) in depth, respectively, and 70 feet (21 m) apart.

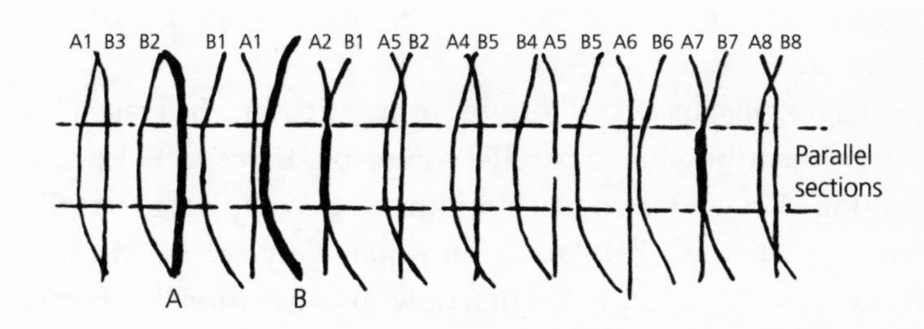

Interactions of the parallels

It is seen that a parallel maze is generated which would fool a dowser of any experience who didn't appreciate what is actually happening. He may conclude that boring be undertaken on the inner parallel of stream 'B' where it happens to coincide with the second parallel of stream 'A'. It is here that the strongest dowsing reaction would be obtained but the point would miss both streams. The strong reactions at 'A7' and 'B7' would, likewise, prove to be grossly misleading since the double strength reactions obtained would also be stronger than the triads of the two streams' bands. Cases such as this are common. It is, however, unlikely that two streams would run exactly parallel for any considerable distance. The solution, therefore, is to delineate several of the parallel reaction bands until one finds some which are not parallel with each other.

Developing a site profile such as that shown in the illustration highlights the problem as it makes the reaction lines of the streams understandable and one can then identify both streams without undue difficulty. It is unlikely that one will need to trace out as many reaction lines as those shown; these simply serve to demonstrate instances of coinciding parallels. One would, probably, notice the lack of agreement in the parallels as soon as the first three, or four, are established.

As the illustration also shows, the parallels cross at certain points and here the reactions will be equal to the sum of both reactions.

In many instances of abortive boring attempts the reason can often be attributable to parallel confusion. In respect of water-finding Guy Underwood's apt phrase often applies to parallel running streams: 'Per Ardua Ad Aqua!' Guy argued strongly against the fallacious belief that dowsers were directly affected by the water itself, and stressed that they are unaffected by, for example, saturated strata, or underground reservoirs, so the dowsing faculty evidently involves more than the water's presence. Guy believed the dowsing reaction is associated with underground streams where the water is in motion, in its natural channels such as rock fissures, subject to friction, under pressure and connecting ultimately with the sea. In support of his belief he pointed out that a skilled water diviner, faced with ten lidded containers of which only one held water, would not achieve better than 'chance' odds in attempting to find the container holding the water.

PRACTICE

For confidence-building practice, try to find an underground stream. Readers may think they are being thrown in at the deep end. But let's be bold and have a go! So, where to start?

As we saw, blind springs generate underground streams, so such a spring is an excellent starting point as these are marked by bronze age burial sites, round barrows, long barrows, solitary standing stones, church altars, fonts and lych gates. The springs generally produce multiple streams so the chance of finding a stream at such locations is highly favourable. At Woodhenge, for example, the blind spring there generates eleven underground streams radiating from the centre.

If a round barrow is selected as the starting point, make a full 360-degree dowsing pass around it. Visualize water running in fissures. Establish how many streams are generated by the spring, then pick one of these and track its course from the barrow for a few hundred paces. This will ensure less interference from the surface patterns of other streams present.

At this point, practise finding all of the phenomena discussed. Be bold. Have the courage of your convictions. Be quietly confident with your newly-found skills, and you may surprise yourself!

Remember the words of the poet Goethe:

> Whatever you can do
> Or dream you can, begin it.
> Boldness has genius, power
> and magic in it

HIGH FREQUENCY VIBRATIONAL DOWSING

The universe is in a constant state of vibration, down to the smallest sub-atomic particles, which vibrate at rates beyond the mind's comprehension. It follows that standing stones, stone circles, medicine wheels and other sacred sites will have characteristic vibrational levels. People, animals, plants and trees, likewise, have vibrational levels and these can be assessed by the use of a biometer scale.

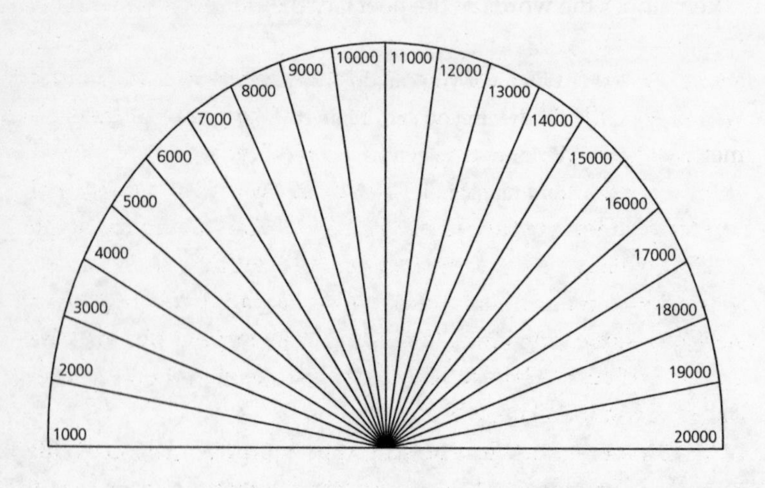

Biometer scale

The scale is graded into segments of gigahertz frequencies. A gigahertz is a frequency level of 1 billion vibrations per second. The following frequency scales apply:

Dowsed Frequencies in Gigahertz	Effects
below 6,500	negative drain on body
6,500 to 8,000	ideal health
above 8,000	too much energy for ideal health
14,000 plus	sacred sites, spiritual power centres

The scale can be made from a photocopy backed with reinforcing card and covered with transparent plastic for use in all weathers.

METHOD OF USE

Place the scale on the ground, or lay it on the palm of the hand. Hold a pendulum above the scale so that the bob is about half an inch over the centre of the base line.

Give the command, 'Show me my personal vibrational level in gigahertz.' Now set the pendulum into a circular 'search' swing. Allow the pendulum to lose its swing momentum and it will eventually begin to swing linearly along one of the segments of the scale, denoting the frequency level.

For sacred sites use the command, 'Show me the vibrational level in gigahertz of this site.' Sites such as Stonehenge are at the 20,000 gigahertz level, or above, often being off the scale.

American readers may wish to assess the levels of Indian standing stones, rocking stones, the Ohio Serpent Mound, the sacred Mulberry Cave in Kansas, the stone chambers of New England and medicine wheels.

The biometer scale is reproduced by kind permission of Bill Burns, a Trustee of the American Dowsing Society and President of the Greater Boston Dowsing Chapter.

8

DOWSING FISSURE SYSTEMS

At the end of the Kennet stone avenue at the Sanctuary – part of the vast Avebury henge site in Wiltshire – there is a complex skein of fissure systems radiating from the centre like the wires of a dartboard.

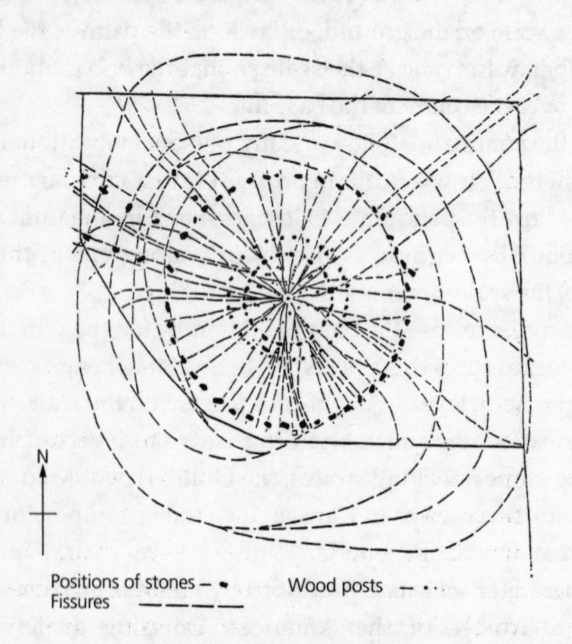

The Sanctuary fissure system

The Sanctuary was once the site of four circular wooden buildings, the first being built in 2900 BC by the settlers on Windmill Hill. Three others were built over the following 200 years. Cylindrical concrete markers indicate their structural postholes. After the wooden building phase, a double concentric stone circle was erected, and oblong concrete markers indicate the individual stones.

PRACTICE

- There are 52 radial fissures, each of varying widths. To find them make a full 360-degree dowsing pass around the outer circle of oblong markers. If dowsing for the leading and trailing edges of each fissure, then 104 dowsing reactions will result. Dowse for the leading edges only, and 52 reactions will result. Use your accuracy indicator in the pass. In this exercise use a single dowsing rod.
- Now dowse for the fissures encircling the Sanctuary.
- To the west of the Sanctuary and outside the outer circle of oblong markers are more oblong markers, showing the positions of the Kennet avenue stones. Dowse for the fissures running within the markers.
- Check at the avenue markers that they mark the width of the Michael current, which courses along the avenue from the henge.
- Now go to the Kennet stone avenue leading from Avebury henge and check for two fissures running parallel along the avenue. Check also for single fissures running parallel with the avenue but outside it. They run outside the stones.
- At Avebury henge, two huge megaliths mark the southern causewayed entrance. There are eight parallel fissures running through the portal stones and into the henge. With these two stones on your left, make a straight dowsing path

across them and detect the leading and trailing edges of the eight parallel fissures.

- Near the portal stones is the stump of a stone which William Stukeley named the 'ring' stone as it had a natural hollow through it. The ring stone has nothing to do with the original breathtaking geometry of the henge. It marks the crossing points of two underground streams. In other words 'sacred space' within the southern circle. Make a 360-degree dowsing pass around the stone and identify the two crossing streams.
- Identify the streams' positive triads.

THE MEDIEVAL MASONS' DESIGN SECRETS

GEODETIC ENGINEERING

Guy Underwood's discovery of the geodetic system of earth energies, in itself, would have assured him a place in dowsing's hall of fame, but his additional discoveries that the geodetic flows and patterns were integrated into the foundation plans of megalithic monuments such as Stonehenge and Avebury henge, was equally seminal. In further research he also found that this neolithic geodetic technology was used by the medieval masonic brotherhood that integrated the ground plans of their cathedrals and churches to conform to the geodetic energies.

The Knights Templars, likewise, set the foundation plans of their churches in line with the geodetic energies.

Every megalithic monument has its own unique 'persona' or 'spirit of place' as do cathedrals and churches. Is this due to the unique geodetic energies integrated into them?

STONEHENGE

Stonehenge, for example, has its main circular features set on geodetic halos: the ditch and bank, the Aubry circular ring of 56 pits, the sarsen stone lintelled circle and the inner ring of blue stones.

The Altar stone and the outlying Heel stone are both set on geospirals. The inner horseshoe arrangement of the huge trilithons is set on a horseshoe flow of energy. Inside the trilithons is a horseshoe arrangement of blue stones and this, likewise, is set on another horseshoe energy flow. Many other features too numerous to list are designed to integrate the earth energies into their designs.

In his research on Stonehenge, Guy Underwood visited the site over two hundred times.

THE MASONIC DESIGN CANONS

In parish church designs the medieval masons had a series of design canons which readers may wish to confirm.

- Altars always set over blind spring geospirals. As we saw, the Stonehenge Altar stone is set over a 7-coil geospiral.
- Towers, fonts and lych gates also set over geospirals.
- Church axis set by energy flows having either 3 or 12 parallel hairlines, which Underwood classified respectively as 'water lines' and 'aquastats'.
- Communion rails set on a transverse aquastat.
- Windows set on transversely flowing aquastats. The masons were adept in the magnificent design of cathedrals. They could have designed parish churches with perfectly symmetrical windows, but chose to place them randomly on aquastat flows. Some churches may have four windows in one wall and two in the other wall, yet this imbalance is seldom noticed and everything seems naturally in order.
- Church boundaries set by aquastat flows.

PRACTICE

Check these masonic design canons at medieval churches.

Let us now look at the geodetic engineering by the masons of a cathedral foundation plan.

CHICHESTER CATHEDRAL

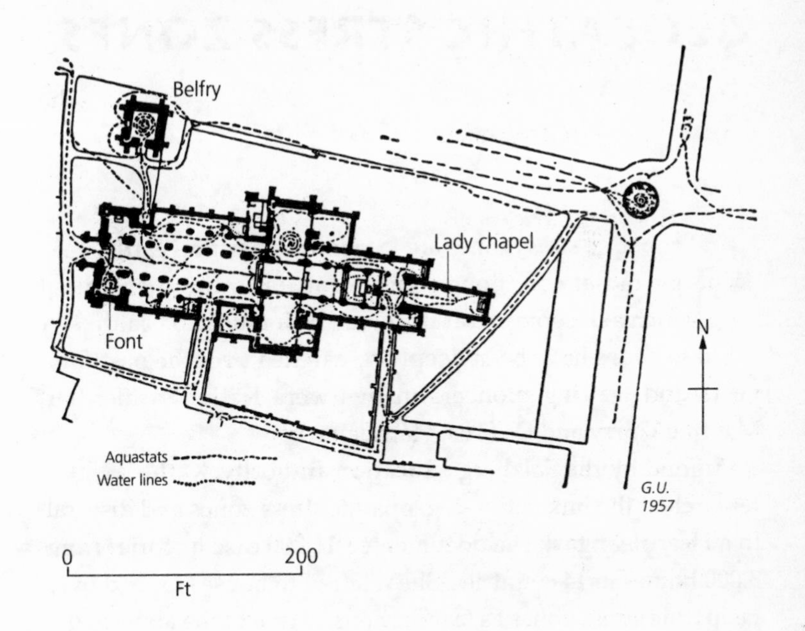

Chichester cathedral

Note how aquastats at the west side door merge into a single flow and set the axis of the cathedral. The spire and font are set over geospirals, and aquastat flows converge on the belfry and form a geospiral.

The widths of the different sections of the cathedral are determined by aquastat flows, as are the boundaries.

GEOPATHIC STRESS ZONES

Geopathic stress zones are locations of harmful earth energy radiations. Long-term exposure to these energies, such as sleeping over them, can be inimical to health.

These zones have been deeply researched over the past fifty years and leading pioneers in this were Käthe Bachler, Dr Manfred Curry and Dr Ernst Hartmann.

Funded by the Salzberg education authority, Käthe Bachler researched the link between geopathic stress zones and disease. In a Herculean task she documented 11,200 case histories from 3,000 homes in 14 countries. She referred to houses located over geopathic stress zones as 'cancer houses' due to the abnormally high incidence of the disease-inducing influences in these homes over several generations of families. Her book gained the support of many doctors, teachers and psychologists who endorsed, unreservedly, her findings. The book outlining her researches, *The Discoveries of a Dowser* (Veritas Verlag), reached its eighth edition in 1984. In his foreword to her book, Dr Lothar R Von Kolitscher wrote: 'We owe much to the author of this book, who worked painstakingly over many years to give us an idea of the extent to which "geopathic fields of disturbance" play a role in sickness and health.'

OTHER RESEARCH

Various other researches have confirmed the same disease-inducing influences of geopathic stress zones. Significant investigations include:

- The university of Heidelberg research
- An analysis in Germany of 5,348 houses by Dr J Hager
- 24,000 experiments with mice by Dr Jenny
- An analysis of 1,000 homes by Dr AJ Kopp
- The Latvian academy of science research

In recognizing this formidable body of research, it behoves us as dowsers to take steps to protect our families, relatives and friends from these damaging earth radiations.

WHAT ARE GEOPATHIC STRESS ZONES?

These zones are energetic radiations from the earth, and are related to:

- underground streams
- geological fault lines
- tunnels and mines
- the crossing points of the global Curry grid

In previous chapters, the practical exercises were compiled to give readers first-hand experience in detecting underground streams, fissure systems and the Curry and Hartmann global grids. Käthe Bachler found that the Hartmann grid had no inimical effects. However, where a Curry grid crossing point coincides with an underground stream or fissure, then the inimical effects are compounded. Another German pioneer, by the name of Voll, believed that 80 per cent of the negative radiations from these sources had 'yin' discharging force fields and 'yang' charging force fields. The 'yang' fields are related to mineral lodes, salt, oil, or ore deposits.

The French researchers, Chaumery and Belizal, defined such radiations as 'negative green' zones and called them 'noxious waves'. They sub-divided negative green zones into alpha waves from geological fault lines and sub-soil cavities, and gamma and beta waves from underground streams. We have already seen how, in later research, Alf Riggs revealed a cocktail of frequencies and electromagnetic field phenomena related to underground streams.

So, what counter-measures can be taken against such geopathic stress zones within our homes?

COUNTER-MEASURES

The first step is to dowse your home for an underground stream coursing under it, fissure systems and Curry grid crossing points. Pay particular attention to beds, armchairs and settees since, if they are located over these geopathic stress zones, they produce long-term exposure to the radiations.

Carefully check for the Curry grid crossing points (which are everywhere on the planet) with grid squares of 3.5 × 3.5 metres aligned northwest and southeast.

If any stress zone is associated with the furniture, then the counter-measure is to move it into neutral zones. Should you be considering purchasing a house, then dowse it for geopathic stress zones before signing a contract.

In Germany, house builders give buyers a certificate confirming that the house is free of geopathic stress zones. In Austria, planning permission will not be allowed until the building plot can be shown to be free of stress zones. This is sensible legislation and is, no doubt, due to Käthe Bachler's findings.

Beyond Austria and Germany, governments blithely ignore detrimental earth energies and little or no publicity is given to their harmful effects.

Countless millions are spent annually in many countries of the world in researching cancers and endeavouring to find cures for the disease. Likewise, countless millions could be saved if the body medical paid heed to Käthe Bachler's pioneering work and researched geopathic stress zones as a cause of cancer and other diseases.

ELECTROMAGNETIC RADIATIONS (EMRs)

EMRs are not geopathic stress zones as such but are an inimical electromagnetic 'smog' pervading the air – and they know no boundaries.

EMRs and their contaminating effects, although having been researched thoroughly have, like the geopathic stress zone research, received very little publicity and governments world-wide remain inert to the findings.

EMR sources arise from:

- all domestic appliances
- television and VDU screens
- electromagnetic pulsing from mains wiring (50 cycles per second in the UK, 60 cycles per second in the USA)
- nearby electric cabling (high or low voltage)
- radio, television and radar signals
- microwave transmissions

EMRs cover a wide range of frequencies from long-wave radio waves to X-rays.

PRACTICE

A television screen radiates two parallel EMR beams which should be avoided by viewing the screen from the side rather than frontally.

With a single rod, make a dowsing pass across the screen to detect the two beams. Twin EMR beams radiate from the rear of the set, so detect these also.

Ensure that the rear end of a television set does not point to an area in the home occupied by family members, such as a dining room or bedroom, for example.

EMR RESEARCH

Of the numerous research studies into EMRs and their detrimental effects, the findings of Dr Hari D Sharma – detailed in 'The Sharma Report' – were significant in showing the relationship between adverse pregnancies and other ailments in workers using VDUs.

LOW POWER EMRS

The leading neuro-scientist, José Delgado, revealed that EMRs as low as one fifteenth of the earth's magnetic field produced alarming results. Chick embryos incubated in such fields emerged grossly deformed and fruit flies suffered lethal genetic mutations. Yet, when we stand under a fluorescent light we receive a much more intensive dose of such energies than that employed by José Delgado in his experiments.

EXTRA LOW FREQUENCY EMRS (ELFs)

Such EMRs range from 1 to 100 Hz (cycles per second). Of the research into the effects of ELFs, the US Navy's 7-year research programme, released in 1984, revealed the harmful effects on humans and animals. They included:

- alterations of cell membranes
- alterations in hormone tissues
- inhibition of bone growth and cell differentiation
- inhibition of kinase production and M(RNA) synthesis
- modification of calcium bonding in cells
- modification in DNA transactions

At the time of writing there are known to exist fourteen giant ELF transmitters around the world and, no doubt, these will be added to over the years. Add to this other ELF sources such as television sets, VDUs and an array of other equipment, all generating ELFs alien to human health. All of this bodes ill for future generations.

The results of this research did not make world headline news.

EFFECTS OF EMRs ON AURAS

People down the ages have claimed to be able to see human auras. Harold Saxon Burr's research in the 1930s showed that the human exterior field – or 'life field' – could be electrically measured. In so doing, Burr gave a scientific endorsement to what occultists called the 'aura'. Later, Kirlian photography showed the scintillating, variegated colours of the auras of humans, animals and plants. By detecting auras we are able to gauge the effects of EMRs on them.

PRACTICE

To dowse for a person's aura, use a single rod in 'search'. With the free arm extended forward, palm raised, move the palm slowly forward to the person's body from a distance of about 3 feet (90 cm). Programme the rod to react when your accuracy indicator touches the aura. The average exterior limit of a healthy aura is 9 to 12 inches (22 to 30 cm) from the body.

Now let us look at how auras can be modified when a person is subjected to geopathic stress zones and EMRs.

AURA MODIFICATION

The aura expands and contracts with varying degrees of health and can be significantly modified by geopathic stress zones and EMRs.

Research by EG Bush revealed the extent of aura modifications in an article he published in *The International Centre for Earth Renewal* (October 1992). The aura shrinkages are shown below:

Type of Stress	Shrinkages to:
underground streams	1 inch (2.5 cm)
Curry grid crossings	1 inch (2.5 cm)
EMRs	1 to 5 inches (2.5 to 12.5 cm)
combined geopathic stress and EMRs	½ inch (1.3 cm)

Here we see the radical nature of the modification of auras with different types of geopathic stress and how combined stresses compound the shrinkage.

PRACTICE

- Dowse a person's aura after they have relaxed, say, in garden. Note the size of the aura. Now let the person be exposed for 2 minutes to the frontal radiation from a TV or VDU screen from a distance of 3 feet (90 cm). Dowse the aura again and note the shrinkage factor. Return to the garden and check the aura at intervals of, say, 5 minutes to determine the time taken for full recovery.

- After the aura has recovered, let the person stand over a Curry grid crossing for 2 minutes, then dowse again to reveal the shrinkage. Check again for the recovery time.
- Repeat this exercise over a Hartmann grid crossing. You will recall that Käthe Bachler did not regard the Hartmann grid as being inimical to health. Note if there is any degree of shrinking.
- Dowse a person's aura after a car journey in which they are exposed to the EMRs from the electrical and electronic fields of the car, which are quite dense in a confined space. Check how long the aura takes to expand to its normal size.

COUNTER-MEASURES

The counter-measures against geopathic stress zones were simple: detect the zones and move the furniture away from them. But what counter-measures can be taken against the all-pervading spectrum of electrical and electronic 'smog', including low power EMRs and ELFs?

In the USA, microcrystals have been developed and housed in various designs to counter intrusive EMRs. Some of these are listed in 'Addresses of Interest', on pages 100–111. In effect the various devices become activated by any incoming alien energy patterns and automatically generate an exact counter-energy pattern.

CONCLUDING COMMENTS

We have seen by the use of our 'sixth sense' that we can discover the invisible – from mundane water pipes to exotic earth energy patterns interlacing the surface of the planet. In this book we have touched on some highly diverse dowsing phenomena but remember, the scope of dowsing is virtually unlimited, the only constraint being the imagination. Dowsing can also be of practical assistance in finding leaks in water pipes or lost objects such as car keys.

For beginners a whole new world emerges once it is realized that the latent 'sixth sense' exists and can easily be triggered into action. The simple exercises in the book were compiled to reveal the scope of dowsing and give beginners an increasing degree of confidence in their dowsing ability.

It is hoped that, by now, most readers will have experienced that exhilarating and 'never-to-be-forgotten' thrill of seeing the dowsing rods swing mysteriously from 'search' to 'found' on detecting a target. But never forget that the rods did not find the target. You did! The rods are merely indicating instruments under your control.

At the end of my dowsing courses, students invariably ask, 'Where do we go from here?' My answer is to practise regularly, daily if possible, and develop your dowsing skills. Specialize in a specific dowsing discipline and work at it until you attain a professional standard. This advice I extend to all readers.

Regular practice will improve your dowsing sensitivity, or psi factor, and your 'credibility' factor. Work particularly on your credibility factor. Make a series of 50 to 100 dowsing passes for various targets that can be verified and note how many times you were right. Keep on making similar passes and note your improvement. Always prepare for the right 'frame of mind' conditions, use visualization of the various targets and always remember to use your personal accuracy indicator. If you missed a target, try to find out what was wrong. Did a passing car disturb your frame of mind, for example?

Many students have taken my advice to heart and some are recognized professionals in different disciplines. One student made an important earth energy discovery and had a book published long before I appeared in print. This particular student attended one of my ten-week courses and I thought he would drop out after the third evening as nothing went right for him and he was highly embarrassed by this. However, things clicked into place during the fourth lesson and in the field work his dowsing was of a high standard. Another formed a successful dowsing society, which has rapidly expanded.

Other students specialized in medical diagnosis with treatments by homeopathy and flower cure remedies. Some became expert at counteracting geopathic stress zones and one appeared twice on a national television network. Prior to joining my dowsing course, these students had never before held a dowsing rod or a pendulum.

My aim in writing *The Principles of Dowsing* was to present the dowsing basics simply and concisely and to expose readers to radically different dowsing phenomena to enhance personal experiences. The chapters on geopathic stress zones and electromagnet radiations were included to show that dowsing has a practical use in safeguarding the health of one's family against the malefic effects of these radiations. Hopefully, my aim has been realized and you, the reader, will be the ultimate judge of this.

My hope is that each reader found dowsing the various exercises to be great fun and will put the newly acquired skill to good use.

Supplements at the end of the book include:

PLACES OF INTEREST

Listed in this section are some of the more important neolithic and bronze age sites in Britain, with ordnance survey map references, and some important sites in America including a stone circle dated to 3000 BC.

This shows that the urge to build stone circles by the neolithic native population of North America was an archetypal custom. America has more sacred spaces than any other country. Like the British neolithics, the American Indians stamped their monuments on the landscape.

Dowsing ancient sites can be a rewarding experience as one gains a deeper insight into the earth energies associated with them, as well as an understanding of the customs and practices of our distant forebears.

ADDRESSES OF INTEREST

This section includes the addresses of worldwide dowsing societies. The American Dowsing Society has 75 affiliated chapters across the States. The British Society of Dowsers has, at the time of writing, 16 independent dowsing societies affiliated to it. Five further independent societies are potential affiliates.

Joining a dowsing society can be of great value in expanding

one's dowsing knowledge by reading society newsletters and journals, attending annual congress gatherings and meetings addressed by experts in a variety of dowsing disciplines, and reading books from their libraries. Most of the societies hold field dowsing trips generally run by experienced leaders who are always willing to help beginners, and from whom one can learn a great deal.

Many web sites can be found by surfing the Internet, including the American and British Dowsing Societies whose Internet site addresses are given here.

BOOKS OF INTEREST

The section includes a bibliography of dowsing-related works, many of which I found to be helpful in my early dowsing days. I was inspired to dowse after reading *The Divining Hand* by the late Chris Bird, and to this American dowsing master I will be forever grateful.

GLOSSARY OF DOWSING TERMS

Aerial Energy An overground energy transmitted between standing stones and individual megalithic monuments. It can be detected by dowsing.

Aquastat A flow line in the geodetic system of earth energies consisting of twelve parallel, individual energetic hairlines of no appreciable width. An aquastat can be several feet in width and its individual hairlines can be detected in a slow, fine dowsing pass. Guy Underwood introduced the word into the earth energy vocabulary and, in so doing, created some confusion, as an aquastat may not necessarily be related to water.

Atavism An inherent ability passed down from remote ancestors. Guy Underwood saw the dowsing ability as a natural sixth sense handed down to us, genetically, from the early hominids. Tom Lethbridge also saw dowsing as a universal ability.

Bionic Charging A stone when held in the hand memorizes the bionic field of the holder for 24 hours before reverting again to 'neutral'. The charge intensity is measured in units of 'petrons'. The charge can be locked in for all time by dynamic or thermal shock.

Bishop's Rule A stream depthing method. The stream's underground depth is equal to the distance from the stream's centre

to the first parallel line of influence. As the parallels move during the day it is not an accurate depthing method.

Blind Spring An underground dome of pressurized water.

Brain Wave Transmissions The brain transmits a range of brain waves such as alpha waves, beta waves, theta waves and delta waves. Much higher frequency waves are also transmitted. The dowsing faculty has been related to brainwaves in the researches of Dr Edith Jurka.

Cardinal Rays Vertical aerials such as standing stones throw out to the main compass points bands of vertically rising electromagnetic energy which is unpolarized. In unsettled weather the cardinal rays swivel by 45° to the mid-compass points and this is known as negative phase. In fine, settled weather the cardinal rays return to their original position. This phenomenon is known as a 'swivel shift'.

Concentric Shells Vertical aerials such as standing stones throw out over the countryside a series of concentric shells created by polarized, electromagnetic, vertically rising energy. Each of the shells is polarized, positive and negative, alternately, and the shells' widths are all equal to the stone's above-ground height. This relationship holds up to the critical height of 16 feet (4.8 m). Stones taller than this will have bands limited to 16 feet widths. When the cardinal rays swivel by 45° the shell polarities all switch from positive to negative and vice-versa. (See *Cardinal Rays*.)

Directional Dowsing Finding the direction of a target by the use of a pendulum or rod. In 'active' directional dowsing the body rotates through a 360° scan with arm outstretched using the index finger as a pointer. When the finger aligns to the target's direction the dowsing instrument reacts to 'found'. In 'passive' directional dowsing no bodily movement is made. The dowsing instrument itself aligns to the target.

Dowsing Instruments Dowsing tools such as pendulums, Y- and L-rods.

Dragon Lines In feng-shui the earth's main energy flows are known as dragon lines. The Michael and Mary earth currents are dragon lines.

Dolmen Chamber A megalithic structure consisting of two or more standing stones supporting a horizontal capstone.

Earth Force The force that Guy Underwood believed to generate the geodetic system of earth energies.

Earth Works Man-made modifications to the earth such as hill forts, henges and man-made hills.

Electromagnetic Spectrum The electromagnetic range of energies spanning long distance radio waves to ultra-high frequency gamma rays.

Feng-Shui An ancient Chinese art of geomancy.

Found Reaction The reaction a dowsing instrument makes when one finds a target.

Frame of Mind A state of mind and body in preparation for a dowsing task in which one visualizes the target in a relaxed condition.

Geodetic System A system of earth energies discovered by the late Guy Underwood. Its features are flows such as water lines, track lines and aquastats plus exotic patterns such as primary halos, secondary halos, geospirals, necklaces and arcs. Geodetic planning was used by the neolithic and bronze age masons, and later by the medieval masonic brotherhood, to integrate the foundation plans of megalithic temples and churches with the geodetic system.

Geomancy The art of recognizing the subtle qualities within a landscape and modifying them so as to create a harmonizing quality of living.

Geomant A geomancy practitioner.

Geospiral One of the geodetic system's most exotic geometric patterns consisting of a main spiral with coils always in multiples of seven up to a maximum of forty-nine. It is joined to a minor spiral, or 'tail' which can be from one-fifth to one-twentieth of the main spiral's diameter. A double, concentric ring of necklaces always accompanies a geospiral. Two geospirals coexist together but of opposite 'hand' and only one can be detected in any moon period. The switch takes place six days after the new or full moon.

Harmonic bands These are lines of influence of differing strengths existing as surface patterns in between an underground stream's parallel lines of influence.

Henge A henge consists of a circular or rectangular earthwork comprising a ditch and bank. Neolithic in origin, they are a peculiarly British construct.

L-Rod A dowsing tool shaped as an L. The short length is gripped, pistol-like, and the longer length is positioned parallel to the ground and pointing forward. The rod can be made of piano wire, fencing wire or a metal coat hanger.

Lattice A stone's construction conforms to a continuous cubic, crystal lattice with atoms at each corner of the cubic structure making a stone, in effect, a single large molecule.

Ley Line Classifications Sig Lonegren, the American dowser, has classified ley lines as follows:

T leys The classical Alfred Watkins ley lines, topographically marked by standing stones, stone circles, moated mounds, cairns, long barrows, round barrows, earthworks, man-made hills and churches.

TAE leys The Saint Michael ley line from Land's End to Hopton on the Norfolk coast targets the Beltane sunrise, is topographically marked along its 300-mile length and has aerial energy passing along it. It is, therefore, a TAE ley.

A leys Many leys align to astronomical events and these he classifies as A leys.

E leys As the standing stones of ley lines transmit aerial energies down the lines, he classifies these as E leys.

Lithon Power The power of a stone equalling the product of its mass and petron charge.

Megalith A standing stone, also known as a monolith.

Negative charge A stone is negatively charged if a pendulum held over it swings counter-clockwise.

Negative dowsers Those who react to an underground stream's negatively-charged zones to either side of the stream.

Nodes:

(a) The crossing of major earth energy flows is defined as a node.

(b) A megalith's transmission bands are also called nodes. These move cyclically with the lunar phases. Five bands are above ground and two below ground. Smaller standing stones have only three above ground bands.

Outlier A megalith standing outside a stone circle.

Parallels A series of parallel lines of influence thrown out to either side of an underground stream and consisting of equally-spaced triads. The parallels attenuate in strength with distance from the stream and move daily on a sun-governed cycle.

Pendulum A dowsing tool consisting of a weight on the end of a twine or fine chain.

Petron Charge A small stone, or pebble, when held in the hand, memorizes the bionic field of the person holding it and is thus charged in units called petrons. The petron was named by Dr J Havelock Fidler.

PSI Factor Relates to dowsing sensitivity. Dr J Havelock Fidler found in his research that his dowsing sensitivity peaked at 4pm on the day of the full moon.

Positive Charge A stone is positively charged if a pendulum held over it swings clockwise.

Positive Dowser A positive dowser is one who reacts to the positive triad of an underground stream's surface pattern known as the stream band.

Programming Assessing the yes/no responses of dowsing tools. One can also, for example, programme a rod to react when an accuracy reference such as the tip of a thumb aligns with the dowsing target.

Recumbent Stone A stone lying on the ground rather than standing.

Reference An accuracy reference is needed for fine dowsing. This could be the tip of the right thumb. (See *programming*.)

Remanence The three-dimensional etheric ghost left by objects or people. The remanence of missing megaliths can be dowsed. People can be tracked by dowsing their remanences.

Search Position This is the prospecting mode when searching for a dowsing object.

Sensors The research of the physicist Dr Zaboj Harvalik showed that the body dowsing sensors are located in the pineal gland and the adrenal glands.

Stream Band An underground stream's energetic surface pattern comprising a central positive triad on either side of which are two zones of equal width and both negative. A dowser can be classified 'positive' or 'negative' according to how he/she reacts to the stream band pattern.

Swivel Shift The swivel movement of a stone's cardinal rays during unsettled weather conditions. The movement is 45°.

Track Line One of the geodetic system's energy flow lines consisting of a double triad. Six dowsing reactions are obtained on crossing a track line at right angles. It is found on ancient trails such as the Ridgeway or on old country roads.

Tracking In dowsing terms tracking means following invisible underground targets such as utilities, or following the remanence trails of people or animals.

Transmission Bands On standing stones these are bands which transmit or receive aerial energy beams.

Triad In the geodetic system three parallel energy hairlines of no appreciable width are defined as a triad.

Trilithons Megalithic assemblies consisting of two vertical stones capped with a horizontal stone. Trilithons form the spectacular horseshoe pattern at Stonehenge.

Tumulus Another name for a bronze age burial barrow.

Visualization The act of visualizing a dowsing objective.

Water Line In the geodetic system a water line is a single triad.

Witness A sample of the target to be dowsed, which is held in the hand during dowsing. The writer has never improved his dowsing technique by using witness aids. The best witness by far is powerful visualization.

Y-Rod A Y-twig cut from a tree is a time-honoured dowsing tool. Plastic versions of the rod can be purchased.

PLACES OF INTEREST

THE BRITISH ISLES

The British Isles are rich in prehistoric sites dating back to the neolithic and bronze ages. Some important sites are listed below giving the ordnance survey map references for each site:

CORNWALL AND DEVON

Site Description	Ordnance Survey Reference
Boscawen-Un Stone Circle	203.412274
The Merry Maidens Stone Circle	203.433245
Nine Maidens Stone Circle	203.435351
Zennor Quoit Dolmen Chamber	203.386324
The Hurlers 3 Stone Circles	200.258714
Trevethy Quoit Dolmen	201.259688
Spinsters' Rock Dolmen	191.700908

SOUTHERN ENGLAND

Site Description	Ordnance Survey Reference
Avebury Henge	173.102699
Silbury Hill	173.100685
West Kennet Long Barrow	173.104677
Maidens Castle	194.670884
Stanton Drew Circle Complex	172.600623

Stonehenge	184.123422
Belas Knap Long Barrow	163.022254
The Rollright Ring	151.295309

NORTHERN ENGLAND

Castlerigg Stone Circle	89.292237
Little Meg Stone Circle	91.576375
Long Meg Stone Circle	91.572373
Arbor Low Henge	119.161636

WALES

Cerrig Duon Stone Circle	160.852206
Parc Le Breos Chambered Cairn	159.537898
Llech-Y-Tripedd Dolmen	145.101432
Clynogg Dolmen	123.407495

SCOTLAND

Ballochroy Megaliths and Kist	62.731524
Lockbuie Stone Circle	49.618252
Torhousekie Stone Circle	83.383564
Cairnpapple Stones and Mound	65.987217
Cullerie Circle and Inner Cairns	38.285043
Loanhead of Daviot Stone Circle	38.747288
Callanish Circle and Avenues	8.213330

ORKNEY ISLES

Knap of Howar Neolithic Village	5.483518
Skara Brae Neolithic Village	6.229187
Midhowe Chambered Tomb	6.372306

AMERICAN SITES

There are 34,000 sacred sites listed by the National Register of Historic Places of America. Readers may wish to dowse the following selected sites.

ANASAZI RUINS

The most prominent of the ancient Anasazi ruins are to be found at Mesa Verde national park in Colorado; Hovenweep National Monument in Utah; Chaco Canyon National Cultural Park and Gila Cliff Dwellings National Monument in New Mexico. Visit the Sun temple at Mesa Verde, which has spectacular views.

THE BIG HORN MEDICINE WHEEL

The Big Horn medicine wheel near Sheridan, Wyoming, is the American Stonehenge. From a central stone cairn, 28 stone spokes radiate outwards to a stone circle. This complex creation is astronomical. At the Summer Solstice, two of the six peripheral stones mark the sunrise and sunset and several other astronomical lines sight major stars. The site is fenced off.

Fifty medicine wheels are scattered across the northern plains, the most striking being a turtle-shaped medicine wheel near Minton, Saskatchewan.

According to Professor RG Forbis of Calgary University, there are more than half a million stone rings scattered around the plains region.

CHIMAYO'S CHAPEL – 'THE LOURDES OF AMERICA'

In the foothills of the Sangre de Cristo mountain range in New Mexico is the chapel of Chimayo – Santurio de Nuestro Senor de Equipulus, said to be a place of miracles. Dowse the altar, font or piscinos for geospirals and check if the church axis is set on an earth energy run comprising 3 or 12 parallel hairlines.

THE HIGH WALLED TEMPLE

The Waha'Ula Heiau temple built in the 13th century, is near the Kalapana entrance to the Volcanoes National Park on Hawaii. Other temple ruins are at Mo'Okini in Hawaii.

THE MONK MOUND

Just across the river from St Louis, Missouri, lies a fascinating complex of earth mounds, Cahokia, created between AD 900 and 1299. The largest earthworks is the Monk Mound, which is 1,000 feet (300 m) long, 700 feet (210 m) wide and 100 (30 m) feet tall. This is the largest prehistoric earthwork construction in the world.

Nearby is a circle of cedar poles known as the 'Woodhenge' of America. Dowse this for a geospiral presence, and check if the circle is set by an earth energy 'halo' comprising 3 parallel hairlines. Check also for aerial ley energy converging on the site.

Woodhenge, near Stonehenge in Wiltshire, was located over a blind spring with its characteristic geospiral surface pattern. Check if this circle of cedar poles is likewise located.

MONTEZUMA CASTLE RUINS

These are near Sedona, Arizona, and are one of a series of ruins along Beaver creek. Check for geospirals, vortices, earth energy runs and aerial energies.

PREHISTORIC STONE CIRCLE

A stone circle believed to date to 3000 BC was discovered on Beaver island in Lake Michigan. The main circle is 397 feet (119 m) in diameter and is constructed with boulders ranging from two to ten feet (60 to 300 cm) tall. Dowse this prehistoric circle

for a central geospiral, the stone's transmission bands, and spin aerial energy around the circumference.

RING MOUNTAIN

In Marin county, California, is the coastal Mywok tribe's Fertility Stone on the summit of Ring mountain in Tiburon.

THE SERPENT MOUND

This great twisting mound lies near Locust Grove, Ohio. The Adena Indians of the Ohio river valley built numerous burial mounds near the Serpent mound in the period 500 BC and AD 1000.

WUPATKI BLOWHOLES

At the Wupatki National Monument in Western Arizona, the ground breathes through caves with winds of up to 30 miles per hour of negative ion-rich air.

GIANT GROUND FIGURES

Giant ground figures created by rock alignments and gravel formations representing humans, animals and ritual symbols are found in Baja, Arizona, California and Nevada.

Around 100 ground figures are in Death Valley, Red Rock Canyon in Kern County, Wild Rose Canyon in Inyo County and the Chocolate Mountains in Imperial County.

The Blyth ground figures are the most famous. The largest figure in this group is 171 feet (51 m) long. Details can be obtained in an information pack from Blyth Chamber of Commerce, California.

Cairns and stone circles are also to be found. Check if the outlines of these figures have attracted earth energy lines comprising 12 parallel hair-lines.

MORE MOUNDS

Some of the famous accessible mounds, temples and effigies are at Etowah Mounds, Georgia; Crystal River Mounds, Florida; Moundville, Alabama; Ocmulgee National Monument Park, Georgia; Moundsville, West Virginia; Indian Temple Mound, Florida; Emerald Mound, Mississippi; Temple Mounds, Wisconsin; Norton Mounds, Michigan; Effigy Mounds National Monument, Iowa; Mounds State Park, Indiana.

As many as 10,000 Indian mounds have been recorded in the Ohio River Valley alone.

MYSTERY SPOTS

Across America there are numerous mystery spots – vortices of energy, which have become tourist attractions. Two of the best known are at Goldhill, Oregon and Santa Cruz, California.

A vortex is a powerful swirl of energy from the ground and it makes a dowsing rod spin wildly out of control. The Indians regarded vortices as holy and treated them as such. The American Dowsing Society and the Canadian Questers can give information on vortex locations.

OTHER RUINS

Check also the Lavanderia ruins at Mission San Luis Rey, California, and the Kiva ruins near Grants, New Mexico.

STONE WORKS

Stone dolmen chambers, altars and crypts are at Danbury, Connecticut; South Woodstock, Vermont; Mystery Hill, Vermont. For more information on stoneworks in Vermont, contact the American Society of Dowsers whose address is given in 'Addresses of Interest'.

ADDRESSES OF INTEREST

Some British readers may wish to join the British Society of Dowsers whose headquarters are at Hastingleigh, Ashford, Kent, TN25 5HW. They have regular lectures, an annual conference, an extensive library, and issue an excellent quarterly journal. Alternatively, you may wish to join one of the independent dowsing groups throughout England, Wales and Scotland who have similar facilities.

Americans may wish to join the American Society of Dowsers who offer similar facilities and services.

In joining such societies you will begin to appreciate, through listening to guest speakers and reading the society's newsletters and journals, the extent of the dowsing discipline and its many aspects of specialization. After passing through the neophyte stage, and establishing an acceptably high credibility factor, you may wish to specialize in a specific dowsing discipline, which could be anything from finding mineral lodes to medical diagnoses, for example. Major General J Scott Elliott taught that there is no such thing as a universal dowser. The professional dowsers may sometimes venture into other aspects of the skill but, in general, having mastered a discipline, they stick to it.

So, find out what you are good at – go for it – and develop your skills.

AUSTRALIA AND NEW ZEALAND

Dowsers Society of New South Wales Inc
PO Box 391
Lindfield
NSW 2070

Dowsers Club of South Australia Inc.
PO Box 2427
Kent Town 5071
South Australia

New Zealand Society of Dowsers and Radionics Inc
PO Box 41-095
St Lukes
Auckland 3

North Tasmanian Dowsing Association
PO Forth
Tasmania 7310

South Tasmanian Dowsing Association
PO Box 101
Moonah
Tasmania

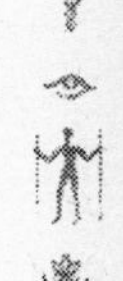

BRITAIN AND IRELAND

The British Society of Dowsers
Sycamore Barn
Hasingleigh
Ashford
Kent TN25 5HW
Phone/Fax: 01233 750253
e-mail bsd@dowsers.demon.co.uk

Website http://www.dowsers.demon.co.uk

There are 21 dowsing societies throughout Britain and the Society can provide information on them. Many are affiliated to the BSD.

Ashdown Dowsers
Ivanhoe
Uckfield Lane
Hever, Kent TN8 7LJ

Bristol Dowsers
8 Ashcombe Crescent
Warmley
Bristol
BS15 5NX

Central Lancashire Society
18 Victoria Street
Abbotts Leigh
Chorley, Lancs PR7 2YX

Devon Dowsers
Corfe Close
High Bickington
Umberleigh
Devon EX37 9AY

East Midlands Group
44 Berry Avenue
Breedon on the Hill
Derbyshire
DE73 1AL

Edinburgh Dowsers
8 Chamberlain Road
Edinburgh EH10 4DN

Greater Manchester Dowsers
5 Sunnymede Vale
Holcombe Brook
Ramsbottom
Bury, Lancashire BL0 9RR

Hampshire Dowsers
2 New Paddock
Howards Lane
Holybourne
Alton
Hants GU34 2HN

Irish Society of Dowsers
8 Thomas Clarke House
Dublin 3
Irish Republic

London and Thameside Dowsers
30 Eastern Avenue
Romford
Essex RM1 4DR

New Forest Dowsers Society
30 Hobbs Park
St Leonards
Ringwood
Hants BH24 2PU

Northamptonshire Dowsers
19 Arnsby Crescent
Moulton
Northants NN3 7SL

Northumbria Dowsers
25 Bournemouth Gardens
Whitley Bay
Tyne and Wear NE26 1QQ

Scientific Research Group
New House
The Crescent
Steyning
West Sussex BN44 3GD

Scottish Dowsing Group
68 Shakespeare Street
Glasgow G20 8JT

Surrey Dowsers
2 Rodney Close
Rodney Road
New Malden
Surrey KT3 5AA

Sussex Dowsers
26 Downview Road
Bognor Regis
West Sussex
PO22 8HQ

Wessex Dowsers
6 Library Road
Parkstone, Poole
Dorset BH12 2BE

West Midland Dowsers
25 Calthorpe Close
Walsall
West Midlands WS5 3LT

West of Scotland Dowsers
10 Queen Margaret Drive
Glasgow G12 8DG

West Wales Dowsing Society
58 Da y Banc
Llanelli
Dyfed SA15 4NS

Wyvern Dowsing Society
48 Goddard Road
Pewsey
Wilts

These addresses are correct at the time of publication. Should any addresses change, the British Society of Dowsers can provide up-to-date information.

CANADA

Canadian Society of Dowsers
2110 Georgeville Road
Magog QC
JIX 3W4

The Canadian Society of Questers
PO Box 4873
Vancouver, BC
V6 B4A6
Web site: http://users.uniserve.com/~questers
(Note: at the time of writing the Canadian Society of Questers and the Canadian Society of Dowsers are considering amalgamating.)

EUROPE

AUSTRIA

Osterreicher Verband für Radiasthesie und Geobiologie
Florianigasse 43/1/12
A-1080 Vienna

BELGIUM

Belgian-Dutch LA Dowsers Association
Mrs N Leunens
Ninoofsteenweg 95
1500 Halle

DENMARK

Miljo- & Jordstraleforeningen Danmark
Henning Juhl
Grænsevej 49
DK 2650 Hvidovre
Copenhagen

FRANCE

Association Française et Internationale
des Amis de la Radiesthésie
c/o Daniel Ville
1 rue Jean Hornet
93170 Bagnolet
Tel: 00 33 1 49 72 88 71

GERMANY

Herold-Verlag Dr Wetzel
Kirchbachweg 16
81479 München

THE NETHERLANDS

Nederlands Genootschap voor Radiësthésue en Radionica
HWJ de Hartog
Postbus 44
1440 AA Purmerend

Dutch-Belgian LA Dowsers Association
Mrs N Martens
Chr van Pallandtlaan 31
2104 SN Heemstede

NORWAY

Norwegian Society of Dowsers
(Norsk Kuistgjenger-forening)
v/Geir AB Wollmann
Zinoberveien
N-0758 Oslo

SWEDEN

Svenska Slagrute för Bundet
Karin Hallberg
Österjärn 2380
85590 Sundsvall

SWITZERLAND

Swiss Association of Radiästhesie
Mr G Heer
Hermenweg 3
CH-5702 Niederlenz

UNITED STATES

The American Society of Dowsers
Danville
Vermont 05825
Phone: 802-684-3417
Fax: 802-684-2565
E-mail: ASD@dowsers.org
Web site: http:/New Hampshire.com/dowsers.org
The Society has 75 Chapters throughout the USA and can provide information on these. Formed in 1961 it has grown to be the world's largest society and will have faster growth with Internet exposure.

OTHER ADDRESSES

The British National Monuments Record Centre covers the nation's ancient archaeology, buildings and maritime sites including a total coverage of England in aerial photography. Their address is:

National Monument Record Centre
Kemble Drive
Swindon
Wilts SN2 2GZ
Phone: 01793 414600

RADIONICS

Radionics uses information from reductional research together with the practice of homeopathy, acupuncture, herbal, flower and gem remedies and many other treatments for illnesses.

The Radionic and Radiesthesia Trust
Maperton
Wincanton
Somerset BA9 8EM
Phone: 01963 32651
Fax: 01963 32626
E-mail: Radionic@cix.co.uk

THE PULSOR

The Pulsor establishes a measure of bioplasmic re-balancing in intensive EMR fields covering low, mid and high frequencies. The device resonates with the physical, emotional and mental life energies.

The intrusion of alien EMRs triggers counter patterns to harmonize the body's natural polarity and energy field.

The Pulsor is in effect an anti-radiation and aura-balancing device, which has a therapeutic effect on the biological functioning of the body.

It is available in designs such as pendants, rings or clip-on attachments. Larger devices counteract EMRs in homes and workplaces. Being passive in operation, the devices have an indefinite life. Pulsors are available in the USA from YAO

International, PO Box 2299, Newport Beach, Ca 926643. They are available in the UK from Regenerative Technology, 22 Greywethers Avenue, Swindon, Wiltshire SN3 1QF.

ENERGY REFRACTORS

These are more sophisticated devices for countering EMRs and are designed to suit individual homes and work places. They block EMRs and ELFs by flooding the environment with positive energies.

The devices are available in the USA from Energy Refractors, 53116 Street, Route 681, Reedsville, OH 45772.

THE TESLAR WATCH

Dr A Pumarich is a world-renowned authority on ELFs. He found that the body operates at its maximum efficiency at a frequency of 7.83 to 8 Hz, this being the natural beat frequency of the planet.

The watch counters ELFs and simultaneously creates the earth's natural beat frequency as a protective barrier.

The Teslar watch is available in the USA from ELF Cocoon International, Route 1, Box 1, St Francisville, Illinois, 62460.

THE SPIRAL OF TRANQUILLITY

The late Wing Commander Beadon was a prominent member of the British Society of Dowsers who, for 25 years, researched into balancing both geopathic stresses and EMRs with crystal technology.

The research culminated in a device called 'The Spiral of Tranquillity' which incorporates eight gemstones of various qualities, colours, vibrational and refractive properties to re-balance intrusive energies. It is available in the UK from 'The Spiral of Tranquillity', PO Box 3072, Corfe Castle, Dorset, BH20 5YT.

THE PREMO DIFFUSER

In the spring issue (1991) of the *American Society of Dowsers Journal,* Charles (Chuck) Premo revealed the details of a diffuser he developed for countering EMRs. It is an easy-to-make, low-cost device containing a coil, two electrical components, batteries and a switch.

The design details and the simple assembly instructions are available on the internet: http://www.hevanet.com/Kennrik. The author has made a diffuser and found it to be effective. For all-round protection keep one in the home and carry another in a pocket or a handbag. My diffuser is housed in a plastic box with dimensions of 3 × 3 × 1½ inches (7.6 × 7.6 × 3.8 cm). The simple assembly, however, for use in the home, need not be housed but could be placed in a drawer or on top of a wardrobe.

BOOKS OF INTEREST

BACHLER, Käthe: *Discoveries of a Dowser*. Veritas Verlag, 10th edition, 1984. English version from Veritas Verlag, Gerald Klonner, Hafenstrasse 1–3, A-4020 Linz, Austria, or the British Society of Dowsers.

The book describes her research into disease-inducing geopathic stress zones which include underground water streams, the crossing points of the Curry global energy grid, and fissure systems. Her research covered 14,000 houses in 14 countries. By 1984 her book had reached its 8th edition.

BARLOW, Bernice: *Sacred Sites of the West*. Llewellyn Publications, USA, 1999.

A delightfully written book, this is a guide to a selection of American sacred centres, including warrior sites, healing centres, vision caves and sites that have inspired all those who hear the 'spirit of place'.

BIRD, Christopher: *The Divining Hand*. Whitford, USA, 1993.

This book by an American dowser is a comprehensive survey of the history of dowsing and will, no doubt, in future years be regarded as a scholarly and classic work. I doubt that it will ever be equalled or bettered. I accidentally stumbled upon the book in a public library. It impressed me so much that I taught myself to dowse. In so doing, it changed my entire career.

BROWN, Simon: *The Principles of Feng-Shui*. Thorsons, 1999.

One of Thorsons' *Principles* books covering a spectrum of subjects, this work introduces the basics of the feng-shui discipline in a no-nonsense, easy-to-read work.

BURL, Aubrey: *Prehistoric Avebury*. Yale University Press, 1979.

An overview of Avebury's ritual landscape by one of the world's leading archaeologists. Aubrey Burl is a prolific author of books on prehistoric sites.

EITEL, E J: *Feng-Shui: The Science of Sacred Landscapes in Old China*. Trubner, 1873.

This book was one of the first to introduce the ancient Chinese discipline to the west.

FARRAR, J A: *Living Perceptions*. Regenerative Technology, 22 Greywethers Avenue, Swindon, Wiltshire SN3 1QF, UK, 1989.

A wide-ranging series of essays on diverse topics including geopathic stress zones.

FEELEY, Dr Helen: *The VDU Operator's Problem Solver*. Planetary Association for Clean Energy, 191 Promenade Avenue, Portage, Suite 600, Hull, Quebec, Canada.

In this book, Dr Feeley, a Canadian optometrist, relates her many encounters with patients suffering from VDU-related illnesses, and how she proceeded to solve these problems.

FIDLER, Dr J Havelock: *Ley Lines* (republished as *Earth Energies*) Thorsons, 1999.

This book covers Dr Fidler's research into the bionic charging of stones with 'petron' charges which gives them 'lithon' power and the ability to transmit an aerial-type energy. He established the wavelength and frequency of the energy in an elegant experiment and, following his laboratory investigations and field work on the standing stones around Loch Shieldaig in Western Scotland, he proposed a coherent ley line theory.

Readers wishing to gain knowledge of the aerial-type energy and more dowsing practice can duplicate his many laboratory experiments on small stones. Fieldwork can then follow at stone circles.

FREKE, Timothy: *The Principles of Native American Spirituality*. Thorsons, 1996.

Another book in the *Principles* series, this is an excellent introduction to the Native American spirituality and view of life. The medicine wheel is their concept of a sacred circle which is the focal point of ceremonial activities as well as being used in everyday life. The wheel refers to the cycle of life from birth to death and to rebirth, the constant movement of which teaches people to change.

GORDON, Rolf: *Are you Sleeping in a Safe Place?* Dulwich Health Society, 130 Gypsy Hill, London, SE19 1PL, or The British Society of Dowsers, 1986.

This book investigates the geopathic stress zones that may exist under beds.

LETHBRIDGE, TC: *The Power of the Pendulum*. Arkana, 1985.

One of the most intriguing books on pendulum dowsing by an Arctic explorer, an archaeologist and a Cambridge don. He taught himself pendulum dowsing and became the doyen of long cord dowsing, taking the discipline into dimensions never before explored. Written in a delightfully rambling style, this book should be read by anyone interested in dowsing. He shows in his 'theory of rates' how long-cord pendulum dowsing can explore other dimensions than our own view of reality.

LONEGREN, Sig: *Spiritual Dowsing*. Gothic Image, 1986.

In this book the American dowser introduces a spiritual dimension to dowsing. The book has been in print continually since 1986.

McAULIFFE, Kathleen: 'The Mind Fields', in *Omni*, volume 7, number 5, February 1985.

This ten-page article describes the invisible energy pulses that affect the behaviour of animals.

MICHELL, John: *The New View Over Atlantis*. Garnstone Press, 1983.

This is a seminal book, which seeded a thousand books being so diverse and original in its thrust. John Michell covers a host of subjects including ley lines, feng-shui, sacred geometry, numerology and the magic squares of antiquity. John is a prolific author and teaches sacred geometry at the Prince of Wales Institute.

MILLER, H and BROADHURST, Paul: *The Sun and the Serpent*. Pendragon Press, Launceston, Cornwall, 1989.

This describes a three-year odyssey in dowsing two great rivers of earth energy from Land's End to Hopton on the Norfolk coast. The twin earth currents Michael (yang) and Mary (yin) intertwine in a balancing act around the celebrated long distance ley line, the Michael ley, which targets the May Day sunrise, an important fire festival event in the ancient calendar known as 'Beltane'. Aligned accurately along the yang and yin currents are over 300 megalithic circles, standing stones, round barrows, long barrows, man-made hills, forgotten shrines, medieval churches, abbeys and priories. At over one per mile along the 300-mile route across southern England, this eliminates coincidental alignments.

MILLER, H: *It's Not Too Late*. Penwith Press, PO Box 11, Hayle, Cornwall TR27 6YF, 1999.

An intensely personal book by the discoverer of the Michael and Mary earth energy currents. In it he explains how a near death experience, and the 'tunnel experience', transformed his life from that of a factory owner to a blacksmith and dowsing healer. The transition makes fascinating reading and culminates in a description of how he discovered that earth energies react to human attention. This is the most riveting part of the book.

The book reveals that dowsing can provide demonstrable proof of the existence of abilities that interlink with everything around us, both seen and unseen. It is a profound journey of the spirit of a master dowser, touching on the world's institutions, commercial, political and religious, which reveals fundamental problems of society and shows that it is not too late for any of us to contribute by changing things in subtle but highly powerful ways.

His personal interactions with the earth energies of the planet are the most exciting aspects of dowsing ever disclosed.

SHARMA, Dr Hari D: *The Sharma Report*. The Planetary Association for Clean Energy, 191 Promenade Avenue, Portage, Suit 600, Hull, Quebec, Canada, 1984.

This book describes the inimical effects on the health of VDU workers by VDU radiations. Also by the same association, *The VDU Operator Problem Solver* by Dr Helen Feeley.

STUKELY, William: *Abury*. London, 1743.

The 18th century antiquarian had a long-lasting love affair with Avebury's shattered megalithic ruins and this book is an overview of his research in the region. Our knowledge of the great Avebury temple is due mainly to his notes and sketches.

SWAN, James A: *Sacred Places*. Bear and Company, Santa Fe, New Mexico, 1990.

Looking at American sacred sites, this book is a fascinating bridge between science and the sacred mysteries of the land and Native American spiritual centres. Dr Swan is one of the leading authorities on Native American customs and beliefs.

UNDERWOOD, Guy: *The Pattern of the Past*. Museum Press, 1969.

This book describes Guy Underwood's discovery of the geodetic system of earth energy flows and patterns in the 1940s and 1950s and how monuments such as Stonehenge were carefully synchronized with the earth energies. This geomantic knowledge was handed down through the neolithic, bronze and iron ages and the final guardians of it were the European medieval masonic brotherhood. Geomantic engineering using the geodetic system was a closely guarded masonic secret, kept even from the church hierarchy.

WATKINS, Alfred: *The Old Straight Track*. Methuen, 1925.

In 1925 Watkins revealed his researches which culminated in his revolutionary thesis that Britain was interlaced with topographically marked linear lines which he called 'ley' lines and shows that the men of prehistory were obsessed with linearities.

WHEATLEY, Dennis: *Dowsing With a Difference*. Braden Press, 67 Swindon Road, Swindon, Wiltshire, SN3 4PU, 1998.

A comprehensive dowsing manual with 18 action-packed appendices.

WHEATLEY, Dennis: *A New View of Stonehenge*. Braden Press, 67 Swindon Road, Swindon, Wiltshire SN3 4PU, 1998.

The book reviews many of Guy Underwood's energy surveys of Stonehenge and shows that the megalithic structure was a lunar observatory in use since 3200 BC to track the moon's 18.61-year metonic cycle. It also explores the sacred geometry at Stonehenge revealing the amazing geometries of John Michell and John Martineau and discusses why the megalithic building customs ended abruptly around 1500 BC across Europe.

WHEATLEY, Dennis: *A New View of the Rollright Ring*. Braden Press, 67 Swindon Road, Swindon, Wiltshire SN3 4PU, 1997.

Reveals that in dowsing terms, this diminutive stone circle on the Oxfordshire/Warwickshire borders is a fascinating centre of activity. Especially intriguing are the constantly changing polarities of the stones, over minutes, hours and days.

ABOUT THE AUTHOR

Dennis Wheatley is the President of the Swindon-based Wyvern Dowsing Society and is a professional dowsing tutor employed by the Wiltshire County Education Authority in their continuing adult education programme. He regularly lectures and writes on dowsing-related subjects and, at the request of national television networks, has made three films on dowsing for earth energy patterns. Additionally, he has made many television appearances. As an electronics engineer, he often brings state-of-the-art scientific instruments to bear on his dowsing research.

Having inherited the research surveys and notes of Guy Underwood, which he has researched over ten years, the author is recognized as the world's leading authority on the geodetic system of earth energies.

DIVINING SACRED SPACE

The author organizes 5-day dowsing vacations in the southwest of England, centred on the village of Blunsdon on the edge of the Cotswolds. *Divining Sacred Space* is a structured course covering some 80 diverse dowsing phenomena suitable for beginners and experienced dowsers. The region is rich in neolithic and bronze age monuments. Visits include:

- The Inner Sanctum at Stonehenge via special access.
- Woodhenge: the site once housed a neolithic wooden cathedral.
- Avebury Henge: the remains of a 3-mile long neolithic temple.
- Silbury Hill: the largest man-made hill in neolithic times.
- Merlin's Mount: the smaller sister of Silbury Hill.
- The West Kennet Long Barrow: the largest chambered tomb in England.
- Wayland Smithy: another large chambered tomb.
- The Rollright Ring: a late neolithic stone circle.
- Medieval churches: in these the masonic brotherhood's secret design canons are explored.

The courses are restricted to ten persons. For further details phone: 01793 723178.